Graphics Concepts for Computer-Aided Design

Second Edition

RICHARD M. LUEPTOW
Northwestern University

PEARSON
Prentice
Hall

Upper Saddle River, New Jersey 07458

Library of Congress Cataloging-in-Publication Data on File.

Editorial Director, ECS: *Marcia J. Horton*
Senior Editor: *Holly Stark*
Associate Editor: *Dee Bernhard*
Editorial Assistant: *Jennifer Lonschein*
Managing Editor: *David A. George*
Production Editor: *James Buckley*
Director of Creative Services: *Paul Belfanti*
Art Director: *Jayne Conte*
Cover Designer: *Bruce Kenselaar*
Art Editor: *Greg Dulles*
Manufacturing Manager: *Alexis Heydt-Long*
Manufacturing Buyer: *Lisa McDowell*
Marketing Manager: *Tim Galligan*

© 2008 Pearson Prentice Hall
Pearson Education, Inc.
Upper Saddle River, New Jersey 07458

Printed in the United States of America

10 9 8 7 6 5 4 3 2 1

ISBN 0-13-222987-0

Pearson Education Ltd., *London*
Pearson Education Australia Pty. Ltd., *Sydney*
Pearson Education Singapore, Pte. Ltd.
Pearson Education North Asia Ltd., *Hong Kong*
Pearson Education Canada, Inc., *Toronto*
Pearson Educación de Mexico, S.A. de C.V.
Pearson Education—Japan, *Tokyo*
Pearson Education Malaysia, Pte. Ltd.
Pearson Education, Inc., *Upper Saddle River, New Jersey*

Contents

ESource Reviewers

We would like to thank everyone who helped us with or has reviewed texts in this series.

Naeem Abdurrahman, *University of Texas, Austin*
Stephen Allan, *Utah State University*
Anil Bajaj, *Purdue University*
Grant Baker, *University of Alaska–Anchorage*
William Beckwith, *Clemson University*
Haym Benaroya, *Rutgers University*
John Biddle, *California State Polytechnic University*
Tom Bledsaw, *ITT Technical Institute*
Fred Boadu, *Duke University*
Tom Bryson, *University of Missouri, Rolla*
Ramzi Bualuan, *University of Notre Dame*
Dan Budny, *Purdue University*
Betty Burr, *University of Houston*
Joel Cahoon, *Montana State University*
Dale Calkins, *University of Washington*
Linda Chattin, *Arizona State University*
Harish Cherukuri, *University of North Carolina–Charlotte*
Arthur Clausing, *University of Illinois*
Barry Crittendon, *Virginia Polytechnic and State University*
Donald Dabdub, *University of CA–Irvine*
Kurt DeGoede, *Elizabethtown College*
John Demel, *Ohio State University*
James Devine, *University of South Florida*
Heidi A. Diefes-Dux, *Purdue University*
Jerry Dunn, *Texas Tech University*
Ron Eaglin, *University of Central Florida*
Dale Elifrits, *University of Missouri, Rolla*
Christopher Fields, *Drexel University*
Patrick Fitzhorn, *Colorado State University*
Susan Freeman, *Northeastern University*
Howard M. Fulmer, *Villanova University*
Frank Gerlitz, *Washtenaw Community College*
John Glover, *University of Houston*
John Graham, *University of North Carolina–Charlotte*
Ashish Gupta, *SUNY at Buffalo*
Otto Gygax, *Oregon State University*
Malcom Heimer, *Florida International University*
Donald Herling, *Oregon State University*
Thomas Hill, *SUNY at Buffalo*

A. S. Hodel, *Auburn University*
Kathryn Holliday-Darr, *Penn State U Behrend College, Erie*
Tom Horton, *University of Virginia*
James N. Jensen, *SUNY at Buffalo*
Mary Johnson, *Texas A & M Commerce*
Vern Johnson, *University of Arizona*
Jean C. Malzahn Kampe, *Virginia Polytechnic Institute and State University*
Autar Kaw, *University of South Florida*
Kathleen Kitto, *Western Washington University*
Kenneth Klika, *University of Akron*
Harold Knickle, *University of Rhode Island*
Terry L. Kohutek, *Texas A&M University*
Bill Leahy, *Georgia Institute of Technology*
John Lumkes, *Purdue University*
Mary C. Lynch, *University of Florida*
Melvin J. Maron, *University of Louisville*
James Mitchell, *Drexel University*
Robert Montgomery, *Purdue University*
Nikos Mourtos, *San Jose State University*
Mark Nagurka, *Marquette University*
Romarathnam Narasimhan, *University of Miami*
Shahnam Navee, *Georgia Southern University*
James D. Nelson, *Louisiana Tech University*
Soronadi Nnaji, *Florida A&M University*
Sheila O'Connor, *Wichita State University*
Matt Ohland, *Clemson University*
Kevin Passino, *Ohio State University*
Ted Pawlicki, *University of Rochester*
Ernesto Penado, *Northern Arizona University*
Michael Peshkin, *Northwestern University*
Ralph Pike, *Louisiana State University*
Dr. John Ray, *University of Memphis*
Stanley Reeves, *Auburn University*
Larry Richards, *University of Virginia*
Marc H. Richman, *Brown University*
Christopher Rowe, *Vanderbilt University*
Liz Rozell, *Bakersfield College*
Heshem Shaalem, *Georgia Southern University*
Tabb Schreder, *University of Toledo*
Randy Shih, *Oregon Institute of Technology*

CHAPTER 1

Engineering Graphics and CAD

Objectives

After reading this chapter, you should be able to

- Describe visual thinking
- Differentiate perspective, isometric, and orthographic projections
- Understand the basis of CAD
- Understand the relationship between design and CAD

OVERVIEW

Engineering designs start as images in the mind's eye of an engineer. Engineering graphics has evolved to communicate and record these ideas electronically or on paper in both two and three dimensions. In the past few decades, the computer has made it possible to automate the creation of engineering graphics using software for computer-aided design, or CAD. Today engineering design and CAD are inextricably connected. Engineering design is communicated visually using engineering graphics produced with CAD software.

1.1 THE IMPORTANCE OF ENGINEERING GRAPHICS

"Visualizing" a picture or image in your mind is a familiar experience. The image can be visualized at many different levels of abstraction. Think about light and you might see the image of a light bulb in your "mind's eye." Alternatively, you might think about light versus dark. Or you might visualize a flashlight or table lamp. Such visual thinking is necessary in engineering and science. Albert Einstein said that he rarely thought in words. Instead, he laboriously translated his visual images into verbal and mathematical terms.

Visual thinking is a foundation of engineering. Walter P. Chrysler, founder of the automobile company, recounted his experience as an apprentice machinist where he built a model locomotive that existed "within my mind so real, so complete, that it seemed to have three dimensions there." Yet, the complexity of today's technology rarely permits a single person to build a device from his own visual image. The images must be conveyed to other engineers and designers. In addition, those images must be constructed in such a way that they are in a readily recognizable, consistent, and readable format. This ensures that the visual ideas are clearly and unambiguously conveyed to others. *Engineering graphics* is a highly stylized way of presenting images of parts or assemblies.

A major portion of engineering information is recorded and transmitted using engineering graphics. In fact, 92 percent of the design process is graphically based. Written and verbal communications along with mathematics account for the remaining eight percent. To demonstrate the effectiveness of engineering graphics compared with that of a written description, try to visualize an ice scraper on the basis of this word description:

> An ice scraper is generally in the shape of a 140 × 80 × 10 mm rectangular prism. One end is beveled from zero thickness to the maximum thickness in a length of 40 mm to form a sharp edge. The opposite end is semicircular. A 20-mm-diameter hole is positioned so that the center of the hole is 40 mm from the semicircular end and 40 mm from either side of the scraper.

It is evident immediately that the shape of the ice scraper is much more easily visualized from the graphical representation shown in Figure 1.1 than from the word description. Humans grasp information much more quickly when that information is presented in a graphical or visual form rather than as a word description.

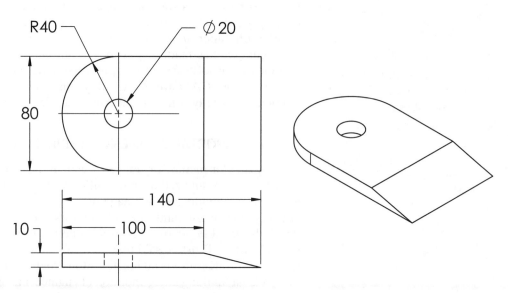

Figure 1.1
Graphical representation of an ice scraper.

Engineering drawings, whether done using a pencil and paper or a computer, start with a blank page or screen. The image in the engineer's mind must be transferred to the paper or computer screen. The creative nature of this activity is similar to that of an artist. Perhaps the greatest example of this is Leonardo da Vinci, who had exceptional engineering creativity devising items such as parachutes and ball bearings, shown in Figure 1.2, hundreds of years before they were reinvented. He also had exceptional artistic talent, creating some of the most famous pictures ever painted, including *Mona Lisa* and *The Last Supper.*

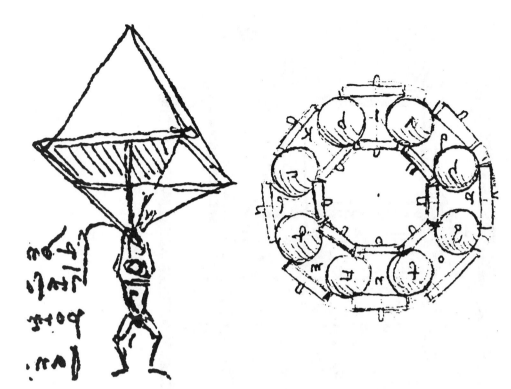

1.2 ENGINEERING GRAPHICS

The first authentic record of engineering graphics dates back to 2130 B.C. based on a statue now in the Museum of the Louvre, Paris. The statue depicts an engineer and governor of a small city-state in an area later known as Babylon. At the base of the statue are measuring scales and scribing instruments along with a plan of a fortress engraved on a stone tablet.

Except for the use of pen and paper rather than stone tablets, it was not until printed books appeared around 1450 that the techniques of graphics advanced. Around the same time, ***pictorial-perspective*** drawing was invented by artist Paolo Uccello. This type of drawing presents an object much as it would look to the human eye or in a photograph, as shown in Figure 1.3. The essential characteristic of a perspective drawing is that parallel lines converge at a point in the distance as parallel railroad tracks seem to converge in the distance. Copper-plate engravings permitted the production of finely detailed technical drawings in large numbers using pictorial perspective. The pictorial-perspective drawings were crucial to the advancement of technology through the Renaissance and until the beginning of the Industrial Revolution. But these drawings could not convey adequately details of the construction of an object. One solution to this problem was the use of the ***exploded view*** developed in the 15th century and perfected by Leonardo da Vinci. The exploded view of an assembly of individual parts shows the parts spread out along a common axis, as shown for the hoist in Figure 1.4. The exploded view reveals details of the individual parts, along with showing the order in which they are assembled.

Figure 1.3
An example of pictorial perspective by Agostino Ramelli in 1588. (Used by permission of the Syndics of Cambridge University Library. All rights reserved. [*The Various and Ingenious Machines of Agostino Ramelli (1588),* translated by Martha Teach Gnudi, Johns Hopkins University Press, 1976. p. 83.])

The Industrial Revolution brought with it the need to more closely tie together the concept of a design with the final manufactured product using technical drawing. The perspective drawing of a simple object in Figure 1.5a shows pictorially what the object looks like. However, it is difficult to represent accurately dimensions and other details in a perspective drawing. ***Orthographic projections***, developed in 1528 by German artist Albrecht Dürer, accomplish this quite well. An orthographic projection typically shows three views of an object. Each view shows a different side of the object (say the front, top, and side). An example of an orthographic projection is shown in Figure 1.5b. Orthographic projections are typically easy to draw, and the lengths and angles in orthographic projections have little distortion. As a result, orthographic drawings can convey more information than a perspective drawing. But their interpretation takes more effort than a pictorial perspective, as is evident from Figure 1.5. French philosopher and mathematician René Descartes laid the foundation for the mathematical principles of projections by connecting geometry to algebra in the 17th century. Much later Gaspard Monge, a French mathematician, "invented" the mathematical principles of projection known as ***descriptive geometry***. These principles form the basis of engineering graphics today. But because those principles were thought to be of such

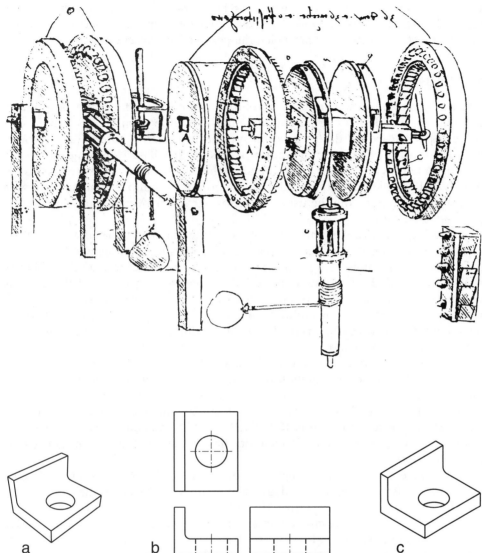

Figure 1.4
Assembled and exploded view of a hoist by Leonardo da Vinci, circa 1500. (Used with permission. Copyrights Biblioteca Ambrosiana, Auth. No. F11/07. All rights reserved. Reproduction is forbidden. [*The Inventions of Leonardo da Vinci*, Charles Gibbs-Smith, Phaidon Press, Oxford, 1978, p. 64.])

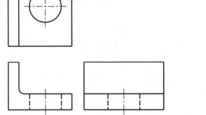

a   b

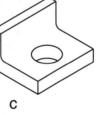

c

Figure 1.5
(a) Perspective projection.
(b) Orthographic projection.
(c) Isometric projection.

strategic importance, they remained military secrets until 1795. By the 19th century, orthographic projections were used almost universally in mechanical drawing, and they are still the basis for engineering drawings today.

The *isometric projection* is used more often today than the pictorial-perspective projection. Historically, it was used for centuries by engravers. Then, in the early 19th century, William Farish, an English mathematician, formalized the isometric projection and introduced it to engineers. The isometric projection simplifies the pictorial perspective. In an isometric projection, parallel lines remain parallel, as shown in Fig. 1.5c, rather than converging to a point in the distance. In addition, the three coordinate axes have the same *metric* (hence the name *iso-metric*). This means that a length unit (say, a centimeter) along one axis has identical length in the drawing along the other two axes. Keeping parallel lines parallel and retaining the same metric along all axes in an isometric projection distorts the appearance of the object slightly. But the distortion in an isometric projection is negligible for objects of limited depth. For situations in which the depth of the object is large, such as an architectural view down a long hallway, the pictorial perspective is preferable. The advantage of the isometric projection, though, is that it is much easier to draw than a pictorial-perspective projection.

1.3 CAD

The introduction of the computer revolutionized engineering graphics. Pioneers in computer-aided engineering graphics envisioned the computer as a tool to replace paper-and-pencil drafting with a system that is more automated, efficient, and accurate. The first demonstration of a computer-based drafting tool was a system called SKETCHPAD developed at the Massachusetts Institute of Technology in 1963 by Ivan Sutherland. The system used a monochrome monitor with a light pen for input from the user. The following year IBM commercialized computer-aided drafting.

During the 1970s, computer-aided drafting blossomed as the technology changed from a scientific endeavor to an economically indispensable industrial tool for design. Commands for geometry generators to create commonly occurring shapes were added. Functions were added to control the viewing of the drawing geometry. Modifiers such as rotate, delete, and mirror were implemented. Commands could be accessed by typing on the keyboard or by using a mouse. Perhaps most importantly, three-dimensional modeling techniques became a key part of engineering graphics software.

By the 1980s, computer-aided drafting was fully developed in the marketplace and became a standard tool in industry. In addition, the current technology of solid modeling came about. Solid models represent objects in the virtual environment of the computer just as they exist in reality, having a volume as well as surfaces and edges. The introduction of Pro/ENGINEER® in 1988 and SolidWorks® in 1995 revolutionized computer-aided design and drafting. Today solid modeling remains the state-of-the-art technology.

What we have been referring to as computer-aided drafting is usually termed *CAD,* an acronym for computer-aided design, computer-assisted drafting, or computer-aided design and drafting. Originally, the term computer-aided design included any technique that used computers in the design process, including drafting, stress analysis, and motion analysis. But over the last 40 years CAD has come to refer more specifically to computer-aided design and drafting. Computer-aided engineering (CAE) is used to refer to the broader range of computer-related design tools.

1.4 DESIGN AND CAD

Inextricably connected with engineering graphics is the *design process* in which an engineering or design team faces a particular engineering problem and devises solutions to that problem. Often the design team includes persons responsible for engineering, product design, production system design, manufacturing, marketing, and sales. The idea is to simultaneously develop the product and the manufacturing process for the product. This is known as *concurrent engineering* or *integrated product and process development*. Key to the success of concurrent engineering is the communication of information. Engineering graphics is one of the primary methods used by concurrent engineering teams to record and transfer information during the design process.

The process of bringing a product to market is shown in Figure 1.6. The process begins with the identification of a market or user need. After this, the design

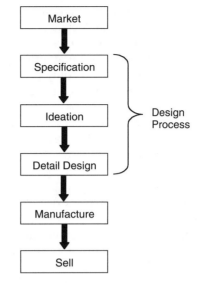

Figure 1.6
The design process.

process is the key to bridging the gap between a user need and the manufacture and sale of a product. The design process can be broken down into three parts as indicated in Figure 1.6. The first part is the ***specification*** of the problem. The ***design specification*** is a list of requirements that the final product must meet, including size, performance, weight, and so on. The second part of the design process is called ***ideation*** or conceptual design. In this phase, the design team devises as many ideas for solutions to the design problem as possible and then narrows them down to the best one based on the specification. In many cases, a designer or engineer will quickly sketch ideas to explore or communicate the design concept to the rest of the design team. These freehand sketches form the basis for the details of the design that are laid down in the third phase of the design process. It is in this last phase of the ***design process***, known as ***detail design***, that CAD is crucial. The conceptual ideas for the product that were seen in a designer's mind or are on paper as rough sketches must then be translated into the visual language of engineering graphics. In this way, the ideas can be understood clearly and accurately by the design team and other designers, engineers, fabricators, suppliers, and machinists. It is in this phase of the design that the nitty gritty details have to be worked out. Should the device be 30 mm long or should it be 35 mm long? How will one part fit with another? What size hole should be used? What material should be used? What manufacturing process will be used to make the part? The number of individual decisions that need to be made can be very large, even for a relatively simple part. Once the engineering drawings have been created, the product can be manufactured and eventually sold.

The use of CAD has had a great impact on the design process. For example, a part may be modified several times to meet the design specification or to mate with another part. Before the advent of CAD, these modifications were very tedious, time consuming, and prone to error. However, CAD has made it possible to make these changes relatively easily and quickly. The connectivity of computers using local area networks then makes the revised electronic drawings available to a team of engineers in an instant. This is crucial as engineering systems become more complex and operational requirements become more stringent. For example, a modern jet aircraft has several million individual parts that must all fit together and perform safely for several decades.

Although CAD had a great impact on making the design process speedier and more accurate, the capabilities of the first few generations of CAD were still limited. Early CAD systems only provided a means of automating the drafting process to create orthographic engineering drawings. The designer or engineer would simply generate a line on the computer screen rather than drawing the line on paper. Current computer graphics software such as "paint" or "draw" programs for personal computers work this way. As CAD became more sophisticated, it helped automate the drafting process on the basis of the "intelligence" of the software. CAD software, lacking such intelligence, required an engineer to draw a pair of parallel lines an exact distance apart by specifying coordinates of the endpoints of the lines. More advanced generations of CAD software permitted an engineer to draw approximately parallel lines using a mouse. Then the engineer would specify a particular distance between the lines and indicate that the lines should be parallel. The CAD software then automatically placed these lines the specified distance apart and made them parallel. However, the major problem with the early generations of CAD software was that the designer or engineer was simply creating two-dimensional orthographic views of a three-dimensional part using a computer instead of a pencil and paper. From these two-dimensional views, the engineer still needed to reconstruct the mind's eye view of the three-dimensional image in the same way as if the drawings were created by hand.

The current generation of CAD software has had a very profound effect on the design process, because it is now possible to create a virtual prototype of a part or assembly on a computer. For example, consider the solid model of a pizza cutter shown in Figure 1.7. Rather than translating a three-dimensional image from the

Figure 1.7
Solid model of a pizza cutter.

mind's eye to a two-dimensional orthographic projection of the object, current CAD software starts with generating a three-dimensional virtual model of the object directly on the computer. This virtual model can be rotated so that it can be viewed from different angles. Several parts can be virtually assembled on the computer to make sure that they fit together. The assembled parts can be viewed as an assembly or in an exploded view. All of this is done in a virtual environment on the computer before the two-dimensional orthographic engineering drawings are even produced. It may sometimes be necessary to produce the orthographic engineering drawings. But these drawings only serve as a standard means of engineering graphics communication, rather than as a tedious, time-consuming task necessary to proceed with the design process.

Professional Success

What Happened to Pencil-and-Paper Drawings?
Solid models and CAD drawings have already replaced pencil-and-paper drawings. Through the 1970s and even into the 1980s many engineering and design facilities consisted of rows and rows of drafting tables with a designer or engineer hunched over a drawing on each table. Engineering colleges and universities required a full-year course in "engineering drafting" or "graphics communication" for all engineering students. Many of these students purchased a set of drawing instruments along with their first-semester textbooks. They spent endless hours practicing lettering and drawing perfect circles.

   Now nearly all of the drafting tables and drafting courses have been replaced by CAD. One can still find a drafting table here and there, but it is not for creating engineering drawings. Most often it is used for displaying a large CAD drawing to designers and engineers. They can make notes on the drawing or freehand sketch modifications on the drawing. The pencil is still an ideal means for generating ideas and quickly conveying those ideas to others. But eventually, all of the pencil markings are used as the basis for modifying the CAD drawing.

   In some companies with traditional products that have not changed for decades (such as a spoon or a chair), pencil-and-paper drawings are being converted into electronic form. In some cases, the original drawing is simply scanned to create an electronic version. The scanned drawing cannot be modified, but the electronic version takes much less storage space than a hard copy. In other cases, the original pencil-and-paper drawings are being systematically converted to CAD drawings, so that they can be modified if necessary. In any case, though, the pencil-and-paper drawing is now just a part of the history of engineering.

			KEY TERMS
CAD	Detail design	Orthographic projection	
Concurrent engineering	Engineering graphics	Pictorial-perspective	
Descriptive geometry	Exploded view	projection	
Design process	Ideation		
Design specification	Isometric projection		

PROBLEMS

1.1 Research and report on an important historical figure in engineering graph-ics, such as Leonardo da Vinci, Albrecht Dürer, Gaspard Monge, René Descartes, William Farish, M. C. Escher, Frank Lloyd Wright, Ivan Suther-land, or Paolo Uccello.

1.2 Using the Internet, search for computer-aided design websites. Report on the variety of software available for CAD and their capabilities.

1.3 Trace the early development of CAD and report on your findings. A particu-larly useful starting point is an article by S. H. Clauser in the November 1981 issue of *Mechanical Engineering*.

1.4 Computer hardware and user-interface development have had a profound effect on the evolution of CAD software. Research and report on the impact of the light pen, the graphics tablet, the direct-view storage tube, raster graphics technology, the work-station computer, the personal computer, or the mouse on the capability and evolution of CAD. (Many textbooks on engineering graphics discuss these items.)

1.5 Outline the design process and indicate how the three steps in the design process would relate to

(a) the design of a suspension system for a mountain bike.

(b) the design of an infant car seat.

(c) the design of headphones for an MP3 player.

(d) the design of a squirrel-proof bird feeder.

(e) the design of a car-mounted bicycle carrier.

(f) the design of children's playground equipment.

(g) the design of a paper towel dispenser.

(h) the design of a manual tool used by a dentist.

1.6 Explain how "paint" or "draw" programs such as Adobe Illustrator, MS Paint, or drawing tools in MS Word differ from CAD engineering graphics software.

CHAPTER 2

Projections Used in CAD

Objectives
After reading this chapter, you should

- Understand the spatial relation between 3-D projections and multiview projections
- Be able to differentiate isometric, trimetric, perspective, and oblique 3-D projections
- Understand how multiview projections are related to the views of the sides of an object
- Know the proper placement of orthographic views
- Know the difference between third-angle and first-angle orthographic projections
- Be able to differentiate the various kinds of working drawings

OVERVIEW

Engineering graphics is a highly stylized scheme for representing three-dimensional objects on a two-dimensional piece of paper or computer screen. This can be accomplished by representing all three dimensions of an object in a single image or by presenting a collection of views of different sides of the object. Working drawings are the practical result of using engineering graphics to represent objects.

2.1 PROJECTIONS

The goal in engineering graphics, whether it is freehand sketching or CAD, is to represent a physical object or the mind's eye image of an object so that the image can be conveyed to other persons. Objects can be shown as ***3-D projections*** or ***multiview projections***. Figure 2.1 shows the handle of a pizza cutter both ways. The 3-D projection clearly suggests the three-dimensional character of the handle, even though it is displayed on a two-dimensional medium (the page). 3-D projections are useful in that they provide an image that is similar to the image in the designer's mind. But 3-D projections are often weak in providing adequate details of the object, and there is often some distortion of the object. For instance, the circular hole through the right end of the handle becomes an ellipse in an isometric 3-D projection.

Multiview projections are used to overcome the weaknesses of 3-D projections. Multiview projections are a collection of flat 2-D drawings of the different sides of an object. For instance, the side and bottom end of the pizza cutter handle are shown in the multiview projection in Figure 2.1. Because there are two views, it is quite easy to depict the details of the object. In addition, taken together, multiview projections provide a more accurate representation of the object than the 3-D projection—a circular hole appears as a circle in a multiview projection. On the other hand, multiview projections require substantial interpretation, and the overall shape of an object is often not obvious upon first glance. Consequently, the combination of the overall

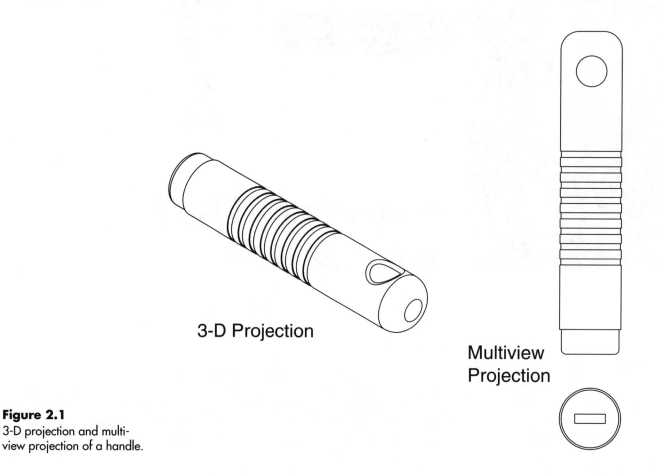

3-D Projection

Multiview
Projection

Figure 2.1
3-D projection and multi-
view projection of a handle.

image provided by 3-D projections and the details provided by multiview projections yields a representation of an object that is best. The shape of the object is immediately evident from the 3-D projection, and the detail needed for an accurate description of the object is available from the multiview projection.

2.2 3-D PROJECTIONS

Two types of 3-D projections are available in most CAD software: isometric and perspective. These two projections of a cube, plus a third less commonly used projection called trimetric, are shown in Figure 2.2. In all three cases, these 3-D projections represent all three dimensions of the cube in a single planar image. Although

Figure 2.2
Isometric, trimetric, and
perspective projections of a
cube.

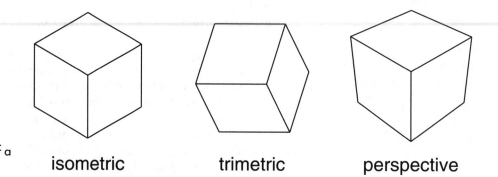

isometric   trimetric   perspective

it is clear in all three cases that the object is a cube, each type of 3-D projection has its advantages and disadvantages.

The *isometric* projection has a standard orientation that makes it the typical projection used in CAD. In an isometric projection, the width and depth dimensions are sketched at 30° above the horizontal as shown in Figure 2.3. This results in the three angles at the upper front corner of the cube being equal to 120° in the plane of the paper. Lines along the edges of the cube, known as *projectors* or *construction lines*, are parallel, so this type of projection is known as a *parallel projection*. Notice that the three sides of the cube are equal in length in the drawing, leading to the term isometric (equal measure). Isometric drawings work quite well for objects of limited depth. However, an isometric drawing distorts the object when the depth is significant. In this case, a pictorial-perspective drawing is better.

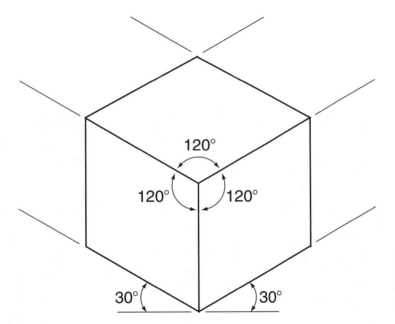

Figure 2.3
Isometric projection of a cube showing parallel projectors.

In general, the *trimetric* projection shown in Figure 2.2 offers more flexibility in orienting the object in space. As with the isometric projection, lines along parallel edges of the cube are parallel. However, in this case, the width and depth dimensions are at arbitrary angles to the horizontal, and the three angles at the upper front corner of the cube are unequal. This makes the three sides of the cube each have a different length as measured in the plane of the drawing—hence the name trimetric. In most CAD software, the trimetric projection fixes one side along a horizontal line and tips the cube forward as shown in Figure 2.2. A *dimetric* projection sets two sides of the cube, usually those of the front face, equal to each other.

A pictorial-perspective, or simply *perspective*, projection is drawn so that parallel lines converge in the distance, unlike isometric or trimetric projections, where parallel lines remain parallel. As shown in Figure 2.4, the projectors converge toward two points, known as vanishing points. This results in *foreshortening*—lines of an object are changed to produce the illusion of the part extending into the third dimension. Perspective projections can also be drawn with a single vanishing point,

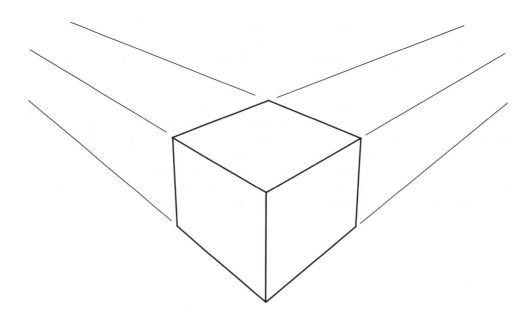

Figure 2.4
Pictorial-perspective projection of a cube showing converging projectors.

which is useful for showing interiors of buildings, or with three vanishing points, which can display perspective for very large objects. Perspective projections are most useful in providing a realistic image of an object when the object spans a long distance, such as the view of a bridge or aircraft from one end or of a tall building viewed from near its base. Generally, small manufactured objects are adequately represented by isometric or trimetric projections.

Two types of pictorial sketches are used frequently in freehand sketching: isometric and oblique. The isometric projection is often used in freehand sketching because it is relatively easy to create a realistic sketch of an object. But the *oblique projection* is usually even simpler to sketch. The oblique projection places the principal face of the object parallel to the plane of the paper with the axes in the plane of the paper perpendicular to one another. The axis into the paper is at an arbitrary angle with respect to the horizontal. Figure 2.5 compares an isometric projection of a cube with a hole in it with an oblique projection of

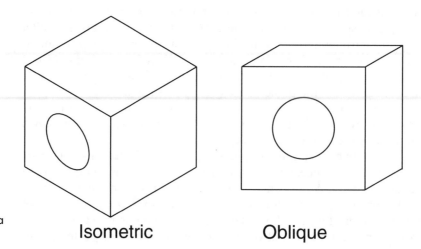

Isometric   Oblique

Figure 2.5
Isometric and oblique projections of a cube with a hole.

the same object. The advantage of the oblique projection is that details on the front face of the object retain their true shape. For instance, the circle on the front face is circular in the oblique projection, while it is elliptical in the isometric projection. This feature often makes oblique freehand sketching somewhat easier than isometric sketching.

2.3 MULTIVIEW PROJECTIONS

The standard means of multiview projection in engineering graphics is the ***orthographic projection***. Although 3-D projections provide a readily identifiable visual image of an object, multiview projections are ideal for showing the details of an object. Dimensions can be shown easily, and most features remain undistorted in multiview projections.

An orthographic projection is most easily thought of as a collection of flat 2-D views of different sides of an object—front, top, side, and so forth. For instance, two orthographic projections could be used for a coffee mug. The front view would show the sidewall of the mug along with the loop forming the handle. The top view would show what one would see looking down into the mug—a circular rim of the mug, the bottom of the inside of the mug, and the top of the handle that sticks out of the side of the mug. Dimensions of the mug could easily be added to the projections of each side of the mug to create an engineering drawing.

One useful way of looking at multiview projections is to imagine a glass box surrounding the object as shown in Figure 2.6. The image of each side of the object can be projected onto the wall of the glass box. Now an observer on the outside of the box can see each side of the object as projected onto each of the six walls of the

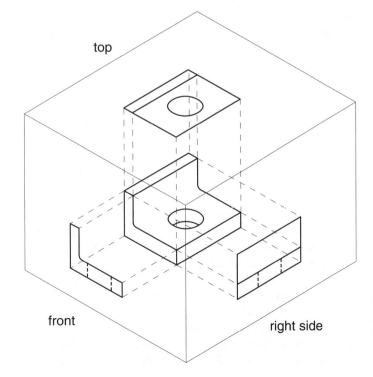

Figure 2.6
Sides of an object can be projected onto an imaginary glass box surrounding the object.

box. Solid lines show the edges evident in the projection, and dashed lines show lines that are hidden by the object. Now imagine unfolding the glass box as if each of the edges of the glass box were a hinge, so that the front view is in the middle. Now the unfolded glass box represents all six sides of the object in a single plane as shown in Figure 2.7. In unfolding the glass box, the top view is positioned above the front view, the bottom view is below the front view, the right-side view is to the right of the front view, and so on. The dimensions of the object remain the same in all views. For example, the horizontal dimension (the width of the object) in the front view is identical to that same dimension in the top view and the bottom view. The views also remain aligned so that the bottom edge in the front view is even with the bottom edge in the right-side, left-side, and rear views. Likewise, the top edges remain aligned. Finally, the same edges in adjacent views are closest together. For instance, the same edge of the object is at the left side of the front view and the right side of the left-side view. This edge in the front view is closest to the same edge in the left-side view.

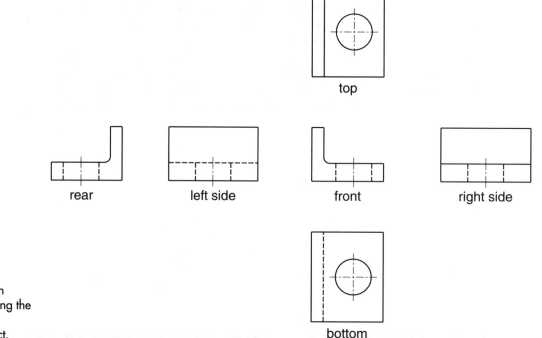

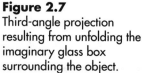

Figure 2.7
Third-angle projection resulting from unfolding the imaginary glass box surrounding the object.

In many cases, three views are needed to represent an object accurately, although in some cases (like a coffee mug) only two views are necessary, and in other cases more than three views are needed to show complex features of the object. It is helpful to select the side of the object that is most descriptive of the object as the front view. Sometimes this may place an object so that what is normally thought of as the front of the object is not shown in the front view of the multiview projection. For example, what is usually described as being the side of a car should be chosen as the front view, because this view is probably most descriptive and easily recognizable as a car. A view of the front of a car (grille, bumper, and windshield) is not as descriptive or as obvious as a view of the side of the car. Furthermore, the object should be properly oriented in the front view. For instance, a car should be shown with its wheels downward in their normal operating position for the front view. The other views that are shown in addition to the front view should be views that best represent features of the object. Normally the minimum number of views necessary to accurately represent the object is used. The standard practice is to use the front, top, and right-side views. But the choice of which views to use depends on the object and which details need to be shown most clearly.

A complication that arises in multiview projections is that two different standards are used for the placement of projections. In North America (and, to some extent, in Great Britain) the unfolding of the glass box approach places the top view above the front view, the right-side view to the right of the front view, and so on, as shown in Figure 2.7. This placement of views is called ***third-angle projection***. However, most of the rest of the world uses an alternative approach for the placement of views. In this alternative approach, the placement of views is what would result if the object were laid on the paper with its front side up for the front view and then rolled on one edge for the other views, as shown in Figure 2.8. For instance, if the object were rolled to the right so that it rested on its right side, then the left side would be facing up. So the left-side view is placed to the right of the front view. Likewise, if the object were lying on the paper with the front view up and then rolled toward the bottom of the paper, it would be resting on its bottom side, so that the top side faces upward. Thus, the top view is placed below the front view. This placement of views, known as the ***first-angle projection***, simply reverses the location of the top and bottom views and the location of the left-side and right-side views with respect to the front view, compared with the third-angle projection. The views themselves remain the same in both projections.

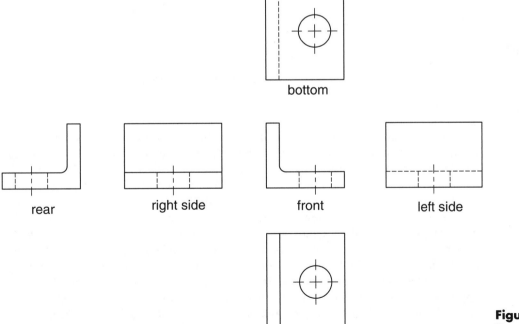

Figure 2.8
First-angle projection of the object.

Although the difference between the two projections is only in the placement of the views, great potential for confusion and manufacturing errors can result in engineering drawings that are used globally. To avoid misunderstanding, international projection symbols, shown in Figure 2.9, have been developed to distinguish between third-angle and first-angle projections on drawings. The symbol shows two views of a solid truncated cone. In the first-angle projection symbol, the truncated end of the cone (two concentric circles) is placed on the base side of the cone, as it would be in a first-angle projection. In the third-angle projection symbol, the truncated end of the cone is placed on the truncated side of the cone, as it would be in a third-angle projection. Usually these symbols appear in or near the title block of the drawing when the possibility of confusion is anticipated. Most CAD software allows the user to choose either first-angle projection or third-angle projection for engineering drawings.

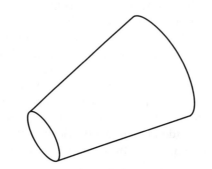

truncated cone

Figure 2.9
Symbols for first-angle projection and third-angle projection based on a solid truncated cone.

first-angle symbol   third-angle symbol

A problem that frequently occurs in orthographic projections is that one of the faces of the object is at an angle to the orthographic planes that form the imaginary glass box. An example is the object shown in Figure 2.10. The circular hole with a keyway (the rectangular cutout on one side of the hole) that is perpendicular to the angled face appears in both the top view and the right-side view. However, it is distorted in both of these views, because it is on an angled plane of the object. An *auxiliary view* is used to avoid this distortion. In this case, a view of the object is drawn so that the angled face is parallel to the auxiliary view plane. The view is based on the viewer looking at the object along a line of sight that is perpendicular to the angled face. Seen from this direction, the circular hole in the auxiliary view appears as a circle without any distortion. As suggested by the projection lines (dash-dot lines) in Figure 2.10, the auxiliary view is projected from the front view in the same way as the top and right-side views are projected. Thus, its position with respect to the front view depends on the orientation of the angled face. It is normal

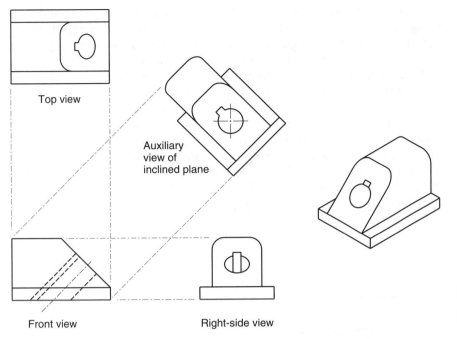

Top view

Auxiliary
view of
inclined plane

Front view

Right-side view

Figure 2.10
Auxiliary view of an
inclined face.

practice not to include hidden lines or other features that are not directly related to
the angled surface in the auxiliary view.

2.4 WORKING DRAWINGS

Several types of *working drawings* are produced during the design process. Initially
freehand sketches are used in the ideation phase of the design process. These are
usually hand-drawn pictorial sketches of a concept that provide little detail, but
enough visual information to convey the concept to other members of the design
team. An example is the isometric sketch of a sheet metal piece that holds the
blade of a pizza cutter, shown in Figure 2.11. The general shape of the object is
clear, although details such as the thickness of the sheet metal and the radius of the
bends in the sheet metal are not included. These conceptual sketches eventually
evolve to final detailed drawings that define enough detail and information to sup-
port production.

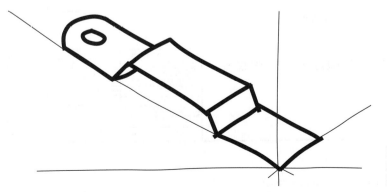

Figure 2.11
Sketch of a sheet metal part
for a pizza cutter.

Detail drawings document the detailed design of individual components using orthographic views. The detail drawing is the final representation of a design that is specific enough so that all of the information necessary for the manufacture of the part is provided. As a result, it is imperative that the detail drawing include the necessary views, dimensions, and specifications required for manufacturing the part. Figure 2.12 shows an example of a detail drawing of the part of the pizza cutter that was sketched in Figure 2.11. The detail drawing includes fully dimensioned orthographic views, notation of the material that the part is to be made from, information on the acceptable tolerances for the dimensions, and a title block that records important information about the drawing. Often an isometric projection is included in the detail drawing to further clarify the shape of the part. Detail drawings provide sufficient detail so that the part can be manufactured based on the drawing alone.

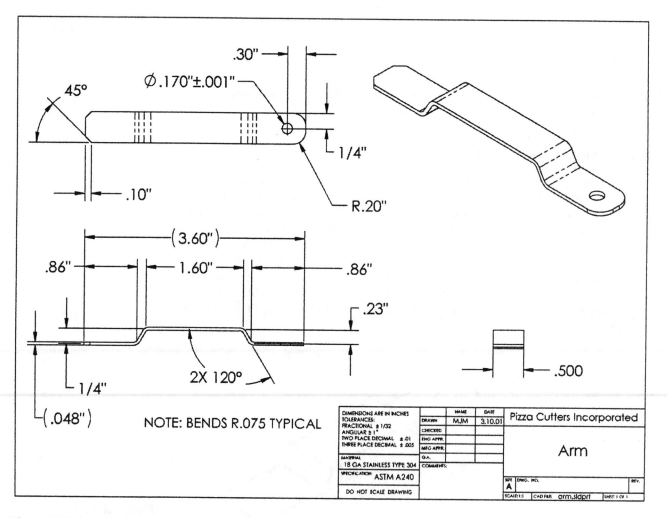

Figure 2.12
Detail drawing of a sheet metal part for a pizza cutter.

Assembly drawings show how the components of a design fit together. Dimensions and other details are usually omitted in assembly drawings to enhance clarity. Several styles of assembly drawings are commonly used. Sometimes the assembly drawing is just an isometric projection of the fully assembled device. But an exploded isometric projection is often helpful to show how the individual parts are assembled, as shown in Figure 2.13 for a pizza cutter. In some cases, a sectioned assembly, or cut-away view, shows how complicated devices are assembled. A cutting plane passes through the assembly, and part of the device is removed to show the interior of the assembly. Numbers or letters can be assigned to individual parts of the assembly on the drawing and keyed to a parts list.

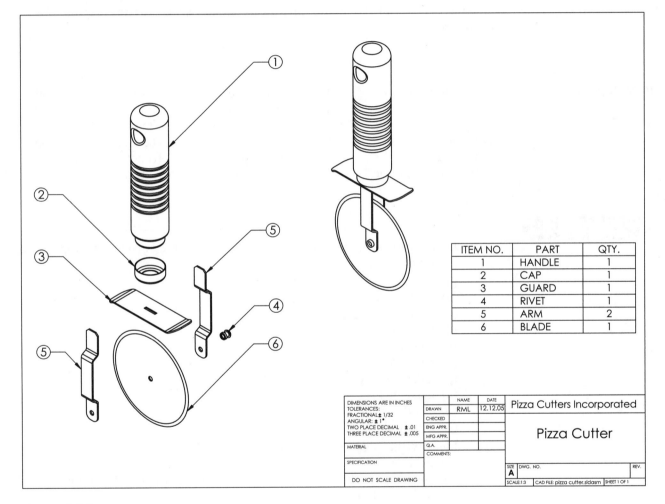

ITEM NO.	PART	QTY.
1	HANDLE	1
2	CAP	1
3	GUARD	1
4	RIVET	1
5	ARM	2
6	BLADE	1

DIMENSIONS ARE IN INCHES		NAME	DATE	Pizza Cutters Incorporated
TOLERANCES: FRACTIONAL± 1/32 ANGULAR: ± 1° TWO PLACE DECIMAL ± .01 THREE PLACE DECIMAL ± .005	DRAWN	RML	12.12.05	
	CHECKED			
	ENG APPR.			Pizza Cutter
	MFG APPR.			
MATERIAL	Q.A.			
	COMMENTS:			
SPECIFICATION				SIZE DWG. NO. REV.
				A
DO NOT SCALE DRAWING				SCALE:1:3 CAD FILE: pizza cutter.sldasm SHEET 1 OF 1

Figure 2.13
Assembly drawing of a pizza cutter.

Finally a *parts list*, or *bill of materials*, must be included with a set of working drawings. The parts list includes the part name, identification number, material, number required in the assembly, and other information (such as a catalog number for standard parts like threaded fasteners). An example is shown in Figure 2.14 for a pizza cutter. The parts list is used to ensure that all parts are ordered or manufactured and brought to the central assembly point.

ITEM	QTY.	PART NO.	DESCRIPTION
1	1	52806	HANDLE
2	1	52825	CAP
3	1	42886	GUARD
4	1	97511	RIVET
5	2	55654	ARM
6	1	56483	BLADE

Figure 2.14
A bill of materials for a pizza cutter.

Taken together, the detail drawings of each individual part, the assembly drawing, and the bill of materials provide a complete set of working drawings for the manufacture of a part.

KEY TERMS

Assembly drawings
Auxiliary view
Bill of materials
Construction lines
Detail drawings
First-angle projection

Freehand sketches
Isometric projection
Multiview projection
Oblique projection
Orthographic projection
Parallel projection

Perspective projection
Projectors
3-D projections
Third-angle projection
Trimetric projection
Working drawings

PROBLEMS

2.1 Describe or sketch the front view that should be used in an orthographic projection of

(a) a stapler.
(b) a television set.
(c) a cooking pot.
(d) a hammer.
(e) a pencil.
(f) a bicycle.
(g) an evergreen tree.
(h) a paper clip.
(i) a coffee mug.
(j) a padlock.

2.2 Identify the projections shown in Figure 2.15 as isometric, trimetric, or perspective.

2.3 For the drawings shown in Figure 2.16, determine whether the multiview projection is a first-angle or third-angle projection.

2.4 Develop a bill of materials for

(a) a pencil.
(b) a squirt gun.
(c) a click-type ball point pen.
(d) a videocassette. (Take an old one apart.)
(e) an audiocassette. (Take an old one apart.)
(f) a disposable camera. (Ask a local photo developer for a used one to take apart.)
(g) eyeglasses.

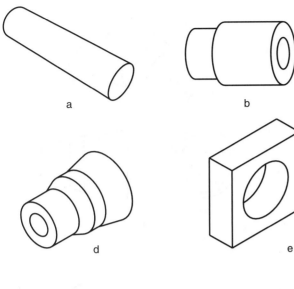
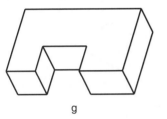
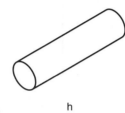
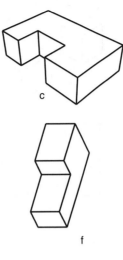

a

b

c

d

e

f

g

h

i

Figure 2.15

(h) a household cleaner pump bottle.
(i) a claw-type staple remover.
(j) an adhesive tape dispenser.
(k) a bicycle caliper brake.
(l) a floppy disk. (Take an old one apart.)
(m) a utility knife.
(n) a vise-grip wrench.

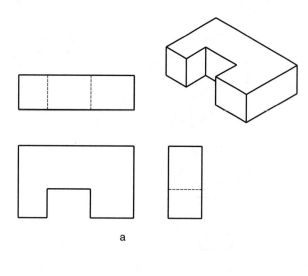

a

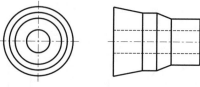

b

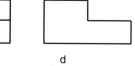

c

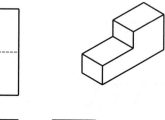

d

Figure 2.16

Freehand Sketching

OVERVIEW

In this chapter you will learn useful techniques for freehand sketching to create both two-dimensional orthographic sketches and three-dimensional pictorial sketches. You will learn how to quickly make rough sketches to convey a concept and how to make more refined sketches of objects that are more complex.

3.1 WHY FREEHAND SKETCHES?

An integral part of the creative design process is *ideation*, the generation of concepts or ideas to solve a design problem. Often freehand sketching can be used to explore and communicate mental concepts that come about in the mind's eye. The process of sketching can solidify and fill out rough concepts. Furthermore, sketching captures the ideas in a permanent form that can be used to communicate the concept to others. In this way, sketches often act as stepping stones to refine and detail the original concept or generate new ideas. Many great design ideas are first sketched on the back of an envelope or in a lab notebook, such as the freehand sketch of an early design of a helicopter by inventor Igor Sikorsky, shown in Figure 3.1.

While computers are the workhorses for engineering graphics, initially generating ideas on a computer display is rare. A more common scenario is sketching an idea on paper and subsequently refining the concept on paper using more rough sketches. This often occurs simply because all that is needed for a freehand sketch is a pencil and a paper. Freehand sketching *quickly* translates the conceptual image from the mind's eye to paper. Engineers often communicate via rough freehand sketches to refine and improve the design. Sketches are much more useful than detailed CAD drawings early in the design process, because they are informal, quickly and easily changed, and less restrictive. It is only after clarifying the design concept by iterating through several freehand sketches that it is possible to draw the object using computer graphics. In fact, often an engineer will sit down to create a CAD drawing of an object using a freehand sketch as a guide.

Figure 3.1
Helicopter inventor Igor Sikorsky's sketch of an early helicopter prototype demonstrates the visual impact of freehand sketching. (Used with permission of the Sikorsky Aircraft Corporation, Stratford, CT. © Sikorsky Aircraft Corporation, 2007. ["Straight Up," by Curt Wohleber, *American Heritage of Invention and Technology*, Winter, 1993, pp. 26–39.])

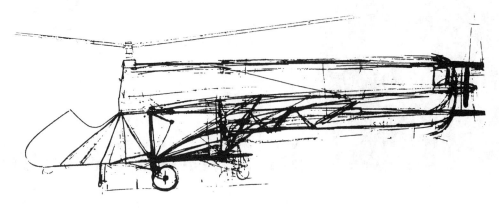

This chapter focuses on the rudimentary elements of freehand technical sketching, because in many ways freehand sketching is the first step in CAD.

3.2 FREEHAND SKETCHING FUNDAMENTALS

Freehand sketching requires few tools: just a pencil and paper. Sometimes it is helpful to use translucent paper, vellum, or tracing paper, to allow overlaying successive versions of a sketch, but this is not necessary. It may be tempting to use straight-edged triangles or rulers for drawing straight lines and a compass to draw circles. But these instruments often slow down the process and distract from the purpose of sketching, which is to create a quick, rough graphical representation of the image in the mind's eye. Generally, sketching has three steps, although the steps are usually subconscious. First, the sketch is planned by visualizing it, including the size of the sketch on the paper, the orientation of the object, and the amount of detail to be included in the sketch. Second, the sketch is outlined using very light lines to establish the orientation, proportion, and major features of the sketch. Finally, sharpening and darkening object lines and adding details develops the sketch.

All sketches are made up of a series of arcs and lines, so the ability to draw circles and straight lines is necessary. A straight line is sketched in the following way. First, sketch the endpoints of the line as dots or small crosses. Then place your pencil on the starting endpoint. Keeping your eyes on the terminal point, use a smooth continuous stroke to draw the line between the points, as shown in Figure 3.2. Nearly horizontal or vertical lines are frequently easier to draw than inclined lines, so it may be helpful to shift the paper to draw the line horizontally or vertically. For long lines, it may be helpful to mark two or three points along the line and use the procedure between consecutive points or to make two or three shorter passes lightly with the pencil before a final darker line.

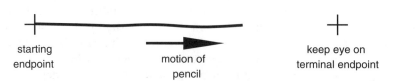

starting endpoint

motion of pencil

keep eye on terminal endpoint

Figure 3.2
Sketching a line.

A circle can be sketched by using the steps illustrated on the left side of Figure 3.3. First, draw light horizontal and vertical lines crossing at the center of the circle. Second, lightly mark the radius of the circle on each line. Finally, connect the radius marks with a curved line to form a circle. Another technique is to lightly draw a square box the same size as the circle diameter, as shown on the right in Figure 3.3. Then lightly draw the diagonals of the box as well as the horizontal and vertical centerlines between the midpoints of the sides of the box. The diagonals and centerlines should intersect at the center of the circle. Mark the radius on the diagonals, and sketch the circle within the box. It is sometimes helpful to mark the radius on the edge of some scrap paper and mark the radius at as many points as desired, in addition to the marks on the centerlines and diagonals. Arcs are sketched in much the same way as circles, except that only a portion of the circle is sketched. It is generally easier to sketch an arc with your hand and pencil on the concave side of the arc.

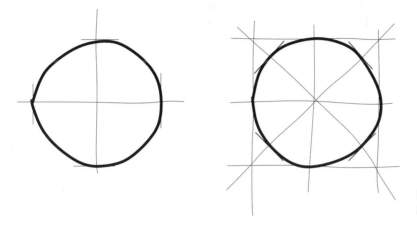

Figure 3.3
Sketching a circle.

3.3 BASIC FREEHAND SKETCHING

Many times, particularly during the conceptual stage of design, it is necessary to immediately communicate a graphical image to others. It has been said that some of the best design engineers are the ones who can sketch an idea clearly in a minute or so. The goal of the sketch in this case is not to show the details of the part, but to provide another person with a clear idea of the concept. For example, a design engineer may need to show a sketch to a manufacturing engineer to get input on the manufacturability of a part. If the concept is at an early phase, CAD drawings would not have been created yet. So the design engineer needs to use a freehand sketch of the part.

The sketch of Sikorsky's helicopter in Figure 3.1 exemplifies the power of freehand sketching. A brief glance at this sketch provides immediate insight into the concept that is being shown. One does not need to study the sketch to know what is being sketched, even if the viewer has never seen the concept before. These quick ideation sketches are not difficult to draw and require no artistic talent, just some practice.

Two types of pictorial sketches are used frequently in freehand sketching: oblique and isometric. The ***oblique projection*** places the principal face of the object parallel to the plane of the paper. The ***isometric projection*** tilts the part so that no surface of the part is in the plane of the paper. The advantage of the oblique projection is that details on the front face of the object retain their true shape. This often makes oblique freehand sketching easier than isometric sketching, where no plane is parallel to the paper. The disadvantage of the oblique projection is that it does not appear as "photorealistic" as an isometric projection. In other words, an isometric projection is similar to what a photograph of the object would look like.

3.3.1 Oblique Sketching

Often freehand sketching begins with light thin lines called ***construction lines*** that define enclosing boxes for the shape that is being sketched. Construction lines are used in several ways. First, the construction lines become the path for the final straight lines of the sketch. Second, the intersections of construction lines specify the length of the final lines. Third, points marked by the intersection of construction lines guide the sketching of circles and arcs. And finally, construction lines guide the proportions of the sketch. This last item is of crucial importance if the sketch is to clearly represent the object. For example, if an object is twice as wide as it is high, the proportions in the sketch must reflect this. Proper proportions of the boxes defined by the construction lines will result in proper proportions of the sketch.

An oblique freehand sketch is easy, since it begins with a two-dimensional representation of the front face of the object. Figure 3.4 shows the steps involved in quickly sketching a part with a circular hole.

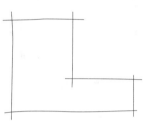

Step 1

Step 2

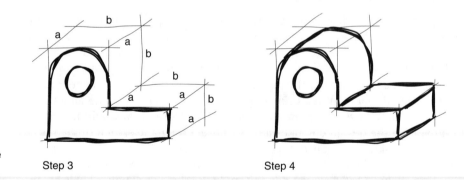

Figure 3.4
Creating a simple oblique
freehand sketch.

Step 3   Step 4

Step 1: Horizontal and vertical construction lines are lightly drawn to outline the basic shape of the main face of the part. This is known as ***blocking in*** the sketch. If you are using a pencil or felt-tip marker, press lightly when drawing the construction lines to produce a thin or light line. If you are using a ball-point pen, draw a single light line.

Step 2: Sketch in the face of the part using the construction lines as a guide. How you sketch the outline of the part depends on the type of pen or pencil that you are using. The idea is to thicken the lines of the part, compared with the construction lines. If you are using a pencil or a felt-tip marker, pressing hard for the outline of the part will result in heavy or dark lines. If you are using a ball-point pen, the line width does not depend much on how hard you press. In this case, the outline of the part is sketched with a back-and-forth motion of the pen to thicken the lines of the part, compared with the construction lines as shown in Figure 3.4. The straight lines are usually sketched first, followed by the arcs. The circle for the hole in the part is added last to complete the face of the part.

Step 3: Sketch *receding construction lines* (lines labeled *a* extending into the plane of the paper, as shown in Figure 3.4) at a convenient angle. All of the receding lines must be parallel to each other and are usually at an angle of 30° to 45° with respect to the horizontal. The receding lines end at the appropriate depth for the object. Then add the vertical and horizontal lines (lines labeled *b* in the figure) at the back plane of the part. This blocks in the three-dimensional box enclosing the object.

Step 4: Sketch in and darken the lines outlining the part. Again, it is usually easiest to sketch in the straight lines first, then the arcs, and finally any details. Because the construction lines are light compared with the outline of the part, they are not erased.

The final sketch, while rough and lacking detail, clearly shows the design intent for the part.

3.3.2 Isometric Sketching

Isometric freehand sketches are somewhat more difficult to master than oblique sketches because no face is in the plane of the paper for an isometric projection. The steps to construct a simple freehand isometric sketch are shown in Figure 3.5.

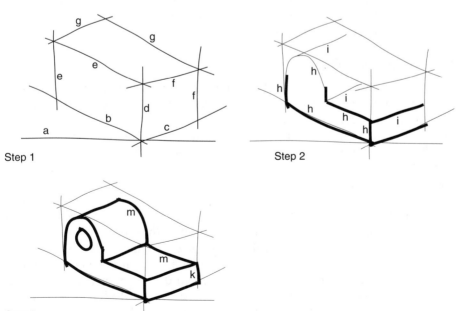

Figure 3.5
Creating a simple isometric freehand sketch.

Step 1: Sketch a light horizontal line (*a*). From this line, draw two intersecting lines at an angle of approximately 30° to the horizontal (*b* and *c*). Then draw a vertical line (*d*) through the intersection of the previous three lines. The three lines labeled *b, c,* and *d* form the isometric axes of the sketch. Next sketch the box to block in the front face of the part (*e*). These lines should be parallel to axes *b* and *d*. Similarly, sketch the lines to block in the right face (*f*), making sure that the lines are parallel to axes *c* and *d*. Finish this step by sketching lines parallel to the axes to complete the box that encloses the part (*g*).

Step 2: The outline for the front face is added by sketching in lines and curves (*h*). Then outline the front face using heavy lines. In this case, a single heavy line that can be produced from pressing hard on a pencil or felt-tip marker is used. Next, lines are sketched to indicate the depth of the features of the front view (*i*). These lines should be parallel to axis *c*. They can be darkened after they are drawn lightly.

Step 3: Finally, a line is added to complete the back corner of the part (*k*). Lines and arcs are added to complete the back face of the part (*m*). Then the hole detail is added. Circular holes appear as ellipses in isometric projections, as discussed in the next section.

The choice of whether to use an oblique projection or an isometric projection is often arbitrary. Because the oblique projection is easier to sketch, it is sometimes preferred. On the other hand, an isometric projection provides a more photorealistic image of the object.

3.4 ADVANCED FREEHAND SKETCHING

The sketching methods described in the previous section were focused on sketches in which the face of the object is in a single plane. Freehand sketching is somewhat more difficult when the face of the object is not in a single plane. The difficulty here is accurately depicting the depth of the object. Oblique and isometric projections are still useful, though somewhat more complicated than those in the previous section. In addition, orthographic projections are also valuable.

3.4.1 Oblique Sketching

The steps leading to an oblique freehand sketch of a more complicated object are shown in Figure 3.6. Because the face of the base of the object and the face of the upper portion of the object are in different planes, it is necessary to begin with a box that encloses the entire object before sketching either face. Some of the construction lines are removed after they are used in this example. This was done here to make the sketch clearer. However, it is not necessary in practice if the construction lines are initially drawn as light lines.

Step 1: To begin, construction lines to form a box that encloses the object are drawn to block in the sketch. Notice that the front and back faces of the box are rectangular with horizontal and vertical sides. The receding construction lines are parallel and set at an angle of 30° to 45° to the horizontal. The easiest way to draw this box is to first draw the front rectangle (*a*). Then draw an identical second rectangle above and to the right of the first rectangle (*b*). Finally connect the corners with the receding construction lines (*c*).

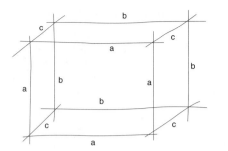

Step 1

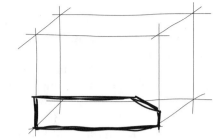

Step 2

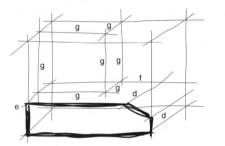

Step 3

Step 4

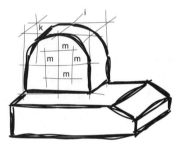

Step 5

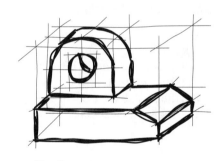

Step 6

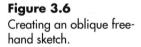

Figure 3.6
Creating an oblique free-hand sketch.

Step 2: Now the front face of the base of the object can be sketched in the front rectangle. The lines are appropriately darkened.

Step 3: Certain features of the front face of the base extend backward along or parallel to the receding construction lines. For example, the lines (*d*) forming the chamfer (the angled cut on the right side of the base) can be sketched parallel to receding lines (*c*). Likewise, the receding line for the upper left corner of the base can be sketched (*e*). Then the base can be finished with a horizontal line on the back face (*f*). Now it is possible to block in the upper rounded portion of the object to create a box (*g*) that encloses the upper protrusion within the larger box that encloses the entire object.

Step 4: The front face of the upper portion of the object can be sketched in this box. Then receding lines corresponding to the chamfer and the left edge of the base can be darkened. In addition, the lines forming the back face can be sketched. Note that the line forming the back edge of the chamfer is parallel to the line forming the front edge of the chamfer. Construction lines (*h*) on the front face of the upper portion are drawn to the center of the circle for the hole.

Step 5: A receding construction line (*i*) extending from the peak of the front face to the plane of the back face is sketched to aid in aligning the curved outline of the back of the upper portion. The back face is identical to the front face except that it is shifted upward and to the right. This results in the left side of the back face being hidden. A darkened receding line (*k*) finishes the left side of the upper portion of the object. Finally, four construction lines (*m*) are sketched to block in the circle for the hole.

Step 6: Now the circular hole can be sketched in and darkened. It may help to draw diagonals to aide in sketching the hole. The back edge of the hole is also added to complete the sketch. The construction lines may be erased, but usually the construction lines are retained if they are made properly as light lines.

Oblique sketching is often aided by the use of graph paper with a light, square grid. The process is identical to that shown in Figure 3.6, but it is easier to keep the proportions correct by counting the number of boxes in the grid to correspond to the approximate dimensions of the part. Graph paper further improves the sketch by helping keep lines straight, as well as more accurately horizontal or vertical.

3.4.2 Isometric Sketching

Isometric freehand sketches of more complex objects start with an isometric box to block in the sketch. Then faces are sketched and additional features are blocked in. Finally details are added. The steps used to construct an isometric sketch are shown in Figure 3.7. Some of the construction lines are removed as the sketch proceeds, to make the sketch clearer for the purpose of this figure. Normally, removing construction lines is not necessary.

Step 1: To begin, sketch a light horizontal line (*a*). From this line, draw two intersecting lines at an angle of approximately 30° to the horizontal (*b* and *c*) and a vertical line (*d*) through the intersection of the previous three lines to form the isometric axes of the sketch. Finish blocking in by sketching lines (*e*) to complete the box so that it will completely enclose the object. Unlike the oblique sketch, it is often better not to sketch hidden construction lines on the back side of the box when blocking in.

Step 2: Block in the front face of the part (*f*) so that the construction line is parallel to the isometric axis. Similarly, sketch the line to block in the right face (*g*). Note that the line on the right face (*g*) intersects the vertical line (*d*) at a lower point than the line on the front face (*f*), because of the chamfer on the right edge.

Step 3: Sketch the left face and the right face, and darken the lines. This completes the faces that are in the front planes of the box. Now sketch in three lines (*h*) parallel to the isometric axis (*c*). The left line (*h*) is the top edge of the base. The middle line (*h*) finishes the chamfer. The right line (*h*) is used to aid in sketching a construction line for the back edge of the base. Finish this step by sketching the construction line (*i*) along the back edge of the base.

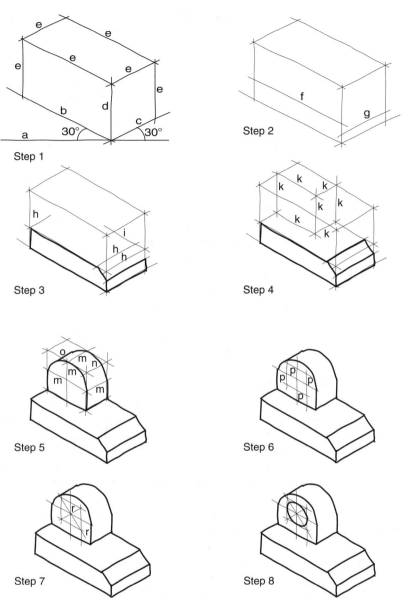

Step 1

Step 2

Step 3

Step 4

Step 5

Step 6

Step 7

Step 8

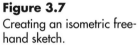

Figure 3.7
Creating an isometric free-hand sketch.

Step 4: Now the face of the chamfer can be darkened and the angled line at the back edge of the chamfer can be added. This completes the angled face of the chamfer. Next the protrusion above the base can be blocked in with seven lines (k). It may help to sketch in the lines on the top face of the protrusion first, followed by the lines on the front face, and finishing with the lines on the right face.

Step 5: The front face of the upper protrusion is sketched first, using light lines. Construction lines (m) are added to help identify the locations of the endpoints of the arc for the front and back faces of the protrusion. The rounded rear face (n) is sketched lightly so that it is identical to the front face, except that part of it is not visible. The line at the top left edge of protrusion (o) is added. Then all lines forming the upper portion of the object are darkened. In addition, the line forming the top edge of the base on the back side is darkened along the construction line (*i*), up to where it meets the protrusion.

Step 6: The details related to the hole are added next. Circles in isometric projections are difficult to draw because they are seen at an angle and appear as ellipses with their major axes at an angle to the horizontal. The center of the hole is where two lines (*m*) intersect on the front face of the upper portion of the object. The lines (*p*) forming the parallelogram to enclose the ellipse for the hole are added. Each side of the parallelogram should be parallel to one of the isometric axes. The sides of the parallelogram should be equal to one another in length.

Step 7: To help in sketching the ellipse, construction lines forming the diagonals of the parallelogram (*r*) are added to the front face of the protrusion. These diagonals, which should be perpendicular to each other, will be along the major and minor axes of the ellipse.

Step 8: Now the ellipse that represents the circular hole can be sketched. A few simple points help in sketching ellipses more easily. The ellipse touches the parallelogram at the midpoints of the sides of the parallelogram. These midpoints are located where the lines (*m*) on the front face intersect with the lines (*p*) of the parallelogram. Start drawing the hole by sketching the gently curved arc between the midpoint at the top of the parallelogram and the midpoint on the right side of the parallelogram. Repeat for the gentle arc between the midpoints on the left side and the bottom side of the parallelogram. Continue by sketching a sharply curved elliptical arc between the midpoints of the parallelogram on the left side and the top side. Finish the hole by sketching the sharply curved arc between the midpoints on the bottom side and the right side. Finally, darken and make heavy the lines outlining the hole and any remaining edges of the part.

Isometric sketching is made substantially easier by the use of isometric grid paper. This paper has a grid of lines corresponding to lines *b, c,* and *d* in Figure 3.7. The procedure for using isometric grid paper is the same as that described above, but using the isometric grid paper keeps the proportions of the part consistent. One simply counts grid boxes to approximate the dimensions of the object. The grid paper also aids in sketching straight lines parallel to the isometric axes.

3.4.3 Orthographic Sketching

In some cases it is necessary to sketch orthographic projection views rather than oblique or isometric projections. Because orthographic views are two-dimensional representations, they are not as difficult to sketch as pictorial projections. But there are several techniques that make freehand sketching of orthographic views easier and more efficient. The process for sketching three orthographic views of the object in the previous two figures is shown in Figure 3.8.

Step 1: Begin by blocking in the front, top, and side views of the object using the overall width, height, and depth of the object. It is usually easiest to start with a ***bounding box*** of the front view that represents the outer dimensional limits of the front face of the object. Then extend

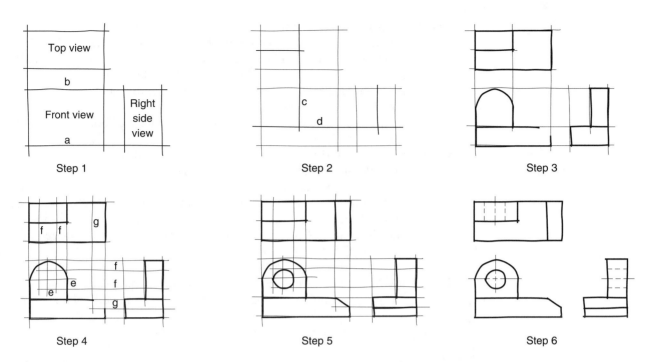

Figure 3.8
Creating an orthographic freehand sketch.

the construction lines between views to properly align the views and maintain the same dimension in different views. For instance, line (*a*) represents the bottom edge and line (*b*) represents the top edge in both the front view and the right-side view. The distance between lines (*a*) and (*b*) is the height dimension in both views. The top view and right view can be thought of in terms of the projection of that side of the object onto the walls of a glass box and then unfolding the glass box to show the projections in the plane of the paper. The space between the views should be large enough so that the drawing does not look crowded and should be about the same for all views. Be sure that the left and right sides of the top view remain aligned with the left and right sides of the front view. Likewise, the top and bottom of the front and right views should be aligned.

Step 2: Block in the upper protrusion in all three views. Note that line (*c*) extends across the top and front views to ensure that the width of the protrusion is consistent in both views. It may help to think again in terms of the glass box. For instance, the top view should represent what the object looks like when viewed through the top wall of the glass box. Line (*c*), which blocks in the upper protrusion, extends to the front view to show the protrusion from that view. Likewise, line (*d*) extends across the front and right-side views to show the upper front edge in both views.

Step 3: The outline of the object is darkened to clearly show the shape of the object in all three views. Care must be taken in darkening lines. For instance, the right corner of the front view should not be darkened, because the detail of the chamfer has not yet been added.

Step 4: Construction lines for the holes and other details are added next. The center of the hole is positioned with construction lines (*e*). Then construction lines (*f*) that block in the hole are drawn. These construction lines extend between views to project the hole to the top view and to the right-side view. Construction lines extending between views (*g*) are also added for the chamfer.

Step 5: Now the hole and chamfer are sketched and darkened to show the completed object.

Step 6: Finally, centerlines (long-dash, short-dash) that indicate the center of the hole are added to all three views. For the top and right views, the centerlines extend along the axis of the hole. In the front view, the centerlines cross at the center of the hole. Hidden lines (dashed lines) that indicate lines hidden behind a surface are also added to the top and right views. Construction lines may be erased as was done in this figure, but that is not usually necessary.

The quality of the sketch can often be improved by using square grid graph paper to keep proportions and act as a guide for horizontal and vertical lines. Some engineers prefer to use a straight-edge to produce a nicer sketch, but this is usually not necessary with practice and sufficient care in sketching.

3.4.4 Sketching Auxiliary Views

When one of the faces of the part is at an angle to the orthographic planes, it may be necessary to sketch an *auxiliary view* so that the features on the angled face are not distorted. The view is based on the observer looking at the object along a **line of sight** that is perpendicular to the angled face. Sketching an auxiliary view seems quite challenging at first, but following a step-by-step approach makes it nearly as easy as sketching a standard orthographic view. Consider the object shown in Figure 3.9, having an angled face with a circular hole and keyway (rectangular cutout). Only the auxiliary view shows the circle without any distortion.

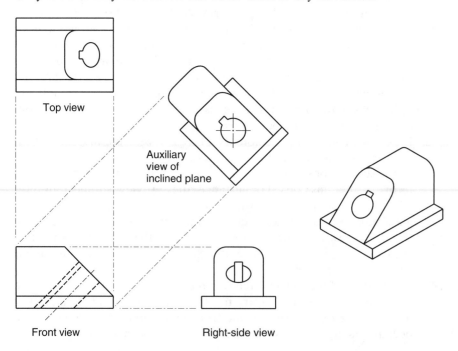

Top view

Auxiliary view of inclined plane

Figure 3.9
Auxiliary view of an inclined face.

Front view

Right-side view

Details of sketching an auxiliary view vary, depending on the nature of the object to be sketched. However, Figure 3.10 shows the steps that would usually be used for the object shown in Figure 3.9, as an example.

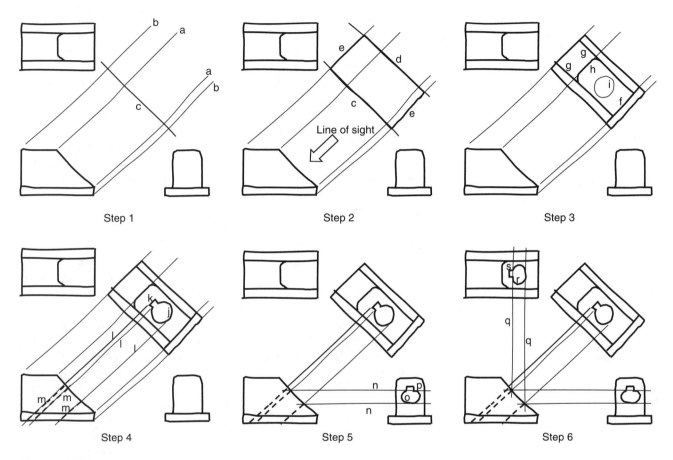

Figure 3.10
Creating an auxiliary view in a freehand sketch.

Step 1: The sketch begins with the three standard orthographic views with a few differences from the way they would normally be done. First, details on the inclined face are omitted from the views until later in the sketching process. In this case, the hole and keyway on the inclined face are not sketched. Second, the three views are separated by a substantial distance. The side view is spaced about twice its width from the front view. Likewise, the top view is spaced about two times its vertical dimension above the front view. This is done to provide space for the auxiliary view. Once these views are sketched, the sketch of the auxiliary view can be done. This begins by sketching two construction lines (*a*) that are perpendicular to the inclined face in the front view and are located at the upper and lower edges of the inclined face. Next, two additional construction lines (*b*) are added. These lines are parallel to the first construction lines and are located at the extreme upper left and lower right edges of the object. These lines will be used to block in the view in the auxiliary plane. The first edge of the object (*c*) is sketched perpendicular to the construction lines (*a*) and (*b*). This line can be drawn any convenient distance from the front view, but usually it is drawn to approximately line up with the lower edge of the top and the left edge of the side view, as shown.

Step 2: Now the outline of the object, as viewed along the line of sight perpendicular to the inclined face, can be blocked in by adding a construction line (*d*). Then the boundaries of the object are added by darkening lines (*c*), (*d*), and (*e*). These are sometimes called **silhouette lines** because they define the outer edges, or silhouette, of the part in the image plane as viewed looking toward the inclined surface in the direction of the arrow indicating the line of sight.

Step 3: The details of other edges evident in the auxiliary view can be added beginning with line (*f*) for the lower edge of the inclined face, followed by lines (*g*) that indicate the inside edges of the flanges, which protrude from either side of the main body of the part (most easily seen as the widest portions of the part in the side view). The curved upper edge (*h*) of the inclined surface can be sketched next. Finally, the circle for the hole (*i*) can be sketched. The hole appears circular in the auxiliary view, which, of course, is the reason for sketching the view in the first place—to show the inclined face and its features without distortion.

Step 4: The hole can be darkened (*j*) and the rectangular keyway (*k*) can be sketched next. Now that the features of the inclined plane have been sketched in the auxiliary view, they can be projected back to the other views. Lines (*l*) that bound the upper and lower portions of the hole and the upper extent of the keyway are drawn parallel to the other construction lines from the auxiliary view so that they extend across the front view. In the front view, these lines correspond to the hidden lines of the hole, which can be darkened as dashed lines (*m*).

Step 5: The upper and lower extent of the hole in the front view can be projected to the side view with construction lines (*n*). Once this is done, it is relatively easy to position and sketch the hole (*o*), which is elliptical in this view, and the keyway (*p*).

Step 6: In a similar way, construction lines (*q*) represent the leftmost and rightmost extents of the hole in the front view that can be projected to the top view. With these lines drawn, the elliptical hole (*r*) and keyway (*s*) are sketched to complete the drawing.

Notice how the auxiliary view is used to more accurately sketch the features (hole and keyway) that are on the inclined surface when they are projected to the front, side, and top views after the auxiliary sketch has been created. Of course, the technique for sketching auxiliary views depends on the nature of the object that is being sketched. For instance, if the inclined surface were on the left edge of the front view instead of the right edge, the auxiliary view would be sketched to the left and above the front view instead of to the right. Likewise, the examples shown in this chapter for oblique, isometric, and orthographic sketches only demonstrate the typical steps that can be used to generate freehand sketches. The exact steps that are used will vary with the details of the object that is being sketched. The steps in freehand sketching become more obvious with practice and experience.

Professional Success

Will Freehand Sketching Ever Become Obsolete?

CAD has almost totally eliminated pencil-and-paper drawings. But what about pencil and paper freehand sketching? Although many computers offer "paint" or "draw" programs, it is unlikely that freehand sketching will disappear soon. Just as it is easier to do a calculation in your head or on a piece of scratch paper rather than finding a calculator and punching in the numbers, it is easier to sketch an image on a piece of paper (or a napkin!) than to find a computer, log in, and start the appropriate program. Pencil-and-paper freehand sketches are quick, efficient, easily modified, and easily conveyed to others. And all that is needed is a pencil and a scrap of paper.

Even if the pencil and paper are totally replaced by laptop or hand-held computers someday, freehand sketching skills will still be useful. Instead of using a pencil on a piece of paper, a stylus can be used on a touch screen. The only difference is the medium. The freehand sketching techniques themselves are unlikely to change much, although sketching software that automatically assists in generating oblique or isometric sketches as they are drawn is a logical enhancement to freehand sketching.

KEY TERMS

Auxiliary view
Blocking in
Bounding box
Construction lines
Ideation
Isometric sketch
Line of sight
Oblique sketch
Receding construction lines
Silhouette lines

PROBLEMS

For Problems 1–9, the items shown in Figures 3.11, 3.12, and 3.13 are 2 inches wide, 1.5 inches high, and 1 inch deep. The holes in Figures 3.11b, 3.11c, 3.11d, 3.12c, and 3.12d are through holes. The hole in Figure 3.12b is through the front face only.

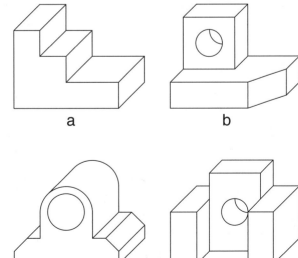

a   b

c   d

Figure 3.11

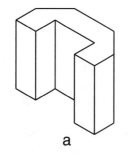

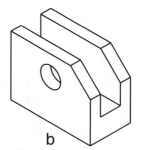

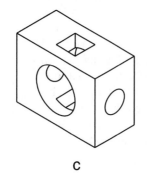

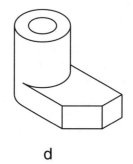

Figure 3.12

a   b

c   d

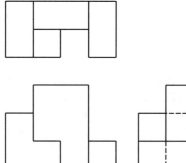

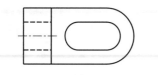

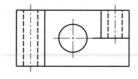

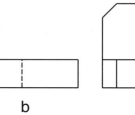

a   b

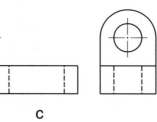

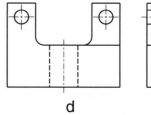

Figure 3.13

c   d

3.1   Create freehand oblique sketches of the objects in Figure 3.11. (The objects are shown as oblique projections, so you must simply recreate the drawing by freehand sketching.)

3.2   Create freehand oblique sketches of the objects in Figure 3.12. (The objects are shown as isometric projections.)

3.3   Create freehand oblique sketches of the objects in Figure 3.13. (The objects are shown as orthographic projections.)

3.4   Create freehand isometric sketches of the objects in Figure 3.12. (The objects are shown as isometric projections, so you must simply recreate the drawing by freehand sketching.)

3.5   Create freehand isometric sketches of the objects in Figure 3.11. (The objects are shown as oblique projections.)

3.6   Create freehand isometric sketches of the objects in Figure 3.13. (The objects are shown as orthographic projections.)

3.7   Create freehand orthographic sketches of the objects in Figure 3.13. (The objects are shown as orthographic projections, so you must simply recreate the drawing by freehand sketching.)

3.8   Create freehand orthographic sketches of the objects in Figure 3.11. (The objects are shown as oblique projections.)

3.9   Create freehand orthographic sketches of the objects in Figure 3.12. (The objects are shown as isometric projections.)

3.10 Consider the pizza cutter shown in Figure 3.14. **(a)** Create a free-hand orthographic sketch of the guard (item 3) in the figure. **(b)** Create a free-hand orthographic sketch of the blade (item 6) in the figure.

3.11 **(a)** Create a freehand isometric sketch of a cube with a vertical circular hole centered in the top surface and extending through the cube. The diameter of the hole should be about one-half the length of the sides of the cube. **(b)** Create a free-hand isometric sketch of a cube with a vertical square hole centered in the top surface and extending through the cube. The sides of the hole should be one-half the length of the sides of the cube and should be oriented so they are parallel to the sides of the cube.

3.12 Create a freehand orthographic sketch of a coffee mug. Only two views are necessary to fully represent the mug.

3.13 Figure 3.15 shows several views of an object. Create a freehand sketch of the auxiliary view of the surface that is indicated.

3.14 Figure 3.16 shows the dimensioned front view and several different corresponding right-side views, each with a horizontal width of 1 inch. Create a free-hand sketch of the orthographic views (front, top, and right side) as well as an auxiliary view of the inclined surface for the corresponding right-side view.

ITEM NO.	PART	QTY.
1	HANDLE	1
2	CAP	1
3	GUARD	1
4	RIVET	1
5	ARM	2
6	BLADE	1

DIMENSIONS ARE IN INCHES
TOLERANCES:
FRACTIONAL ± 1/32
ANGULAR: ± 1°
TWO PLACE DECIMAL ± .01
THREE PLACE DECIMAL ± .005

MATERIAL

SPECIFICATION

DO NOT SCALE DRAWING

	NAME	DATE
DRAWN	RML	12.12.05
CHECKED		
ENG APPR.		
MFG APPR.		
Q.A.		
COMMENTS:		

Pizza Cutters Incorporated

Pizza Cutter

SIZE **A** DWG. NO. REV.

SCALE:1:3 CAD FILE: pizza cutter.sldasm SHEET 1 OF 1

Figure 3.14

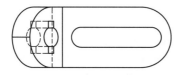

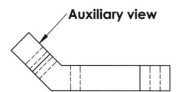

Auxiliary view

Figure 3.15

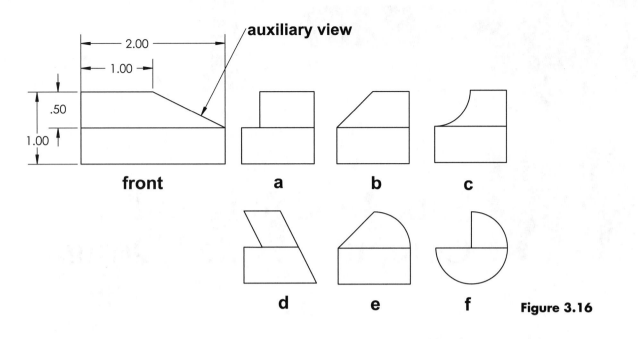

Figure 3.16

Solid Modeling and Computer-Aided Design

OVERVIEW

Several different models for representing a part's geometry have been used in CAD, including 2-D models and 3-D wireframe and surface models. However, solid modeling is the current state of the art in CAD. Solid modeling has the inherent advantage of more accurately representing the "design intent" of the part that is modeled.

4.1 CAD MODELS

A CAD *model* is a computer representation of an object or part. It can be thought of as a "virtual" part in that it exists only as a computer image. The model is an engineering document of record. It contains all of the design information, including the geometry, dimensions, tolerances, materials, and manufacturing information. A CAD model replaces the paper blueprints and engineering drawings used a few decades ago.

The simplest model used in CAD is a *2-D model*. This model is essentially the computer graphics equivalent of an orthographic projection created using a pencil and paper, as shown in Figure 4.1. A 2-D model represents a three-dimensional object with several views, each showing one side of the object projected onto a plane. On the computer, a 2-D model appears as lines and curves on a flat surface, and it is up to the engineer or designer to interpret several views to create a mind's eye image of the three-dimensional object. The CAD software electronically stores the 2-D model as several views but does not inherently "know" that the views can be connected to one another to form a three-dimensional object.

A *2 1/2-D model* has a third dimension that is recognized by the CAD software, but the third dimension is simply an extrusion of a two-dimensional shape. In this case, the CAD software electronically stores the cross-sectional shape of the object and the depth that it is *extruded*, or stretched, in the third dimension. Thus, the only objects that can be represented using a 2 1/2-D model are those that have a constant cross section. For instance, the simple shape

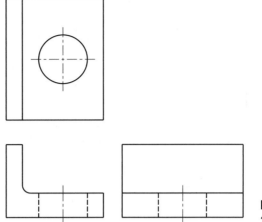

Figure 4.1
2-D model of an object.

shown in Figure 4.2 is the 2 1/2-D model of the object shown using a 2-D model in Figure 4.1 without the hole. The object, including the hole, cannot be represented as a 2 1/2-D model because the hole results in a change in the cross section. A 2 1/2-D model could be used to represent a shape such as an I-beam or C-channel.

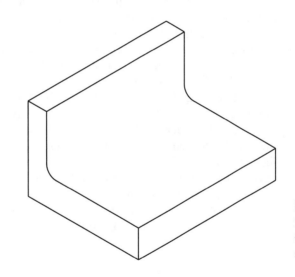

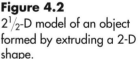

Figure 4.2
2$\frac{1}{2}$-D model of an object formed by extruding a 2-D shape.

A **3-D model** is the most general model used in CAD software. In this case, the CAD software electronically stores the entire three-dimensional shape of the object. Most simply, one can think of the software storing the three-dimensional co-ordinates of various points on the object and then defining how these points are connected. Of course, a two-dimensional drawing representing the orthographic views of the object can be automatically created from the 3-D model. The current generation of CAD software is based on 3-D models.

The simplest 3-D model is a **wireframe model**. Figure 4.3a shows a wireframe representation of the object that we have been considering. In a wireframe model, only edges of the object are represented. Thus, the CAD software needs to store the locations of the vertices (intersections of lines) and information about which vertices are to be connected to each other by lines. A circle or curved section can be represented by a series of closely spaced vertices with linear edges connecting them or as an arc defined by a center, radius, and end points. Before more powerful

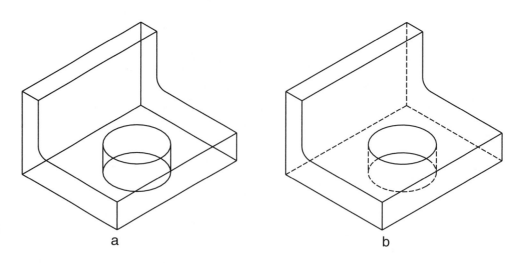

a   b

Figure 4.3
(a) 3-D wireframe model.
(b) 3-D wireframe model
with hidden lines shown as
dashed lines.

computers were available, the low storage requirements of a wireframe model made it quite popular. The problem inherent in a wireframe representation is quite clear in Figure 4.3a—it is difficult to interpret the drawing because all of the edges are visible. In fact, there are many situations where a wireframe representation cannot be unambiguously interpreted because it is not clear which lines would remain hidden if the surfaces of the part were filled in. This problem can be solved using various methods to remove "hidden lines" from the wireframe. This is tricky because the CAD software has to first determine how the edges of the wireframe form a surface and then determine whether that surface hides any lines. Figure 4.3b shows the object with the hidden lines shown as dashed lines to indicate that they are behind a surface. 3-D models not based on wireframes are able to deal with hidden lines more effectively and offer other advantages.

A 3-D *surface model* defines the object in terms of surfaces such as plates (flat) and shells (curved) in addition to edges. This makes it easy to determine whether a line or surface is hidden, because the surfaces are defined. Using a surface model also permits the construction of smoothly curved surfaces, such as a circular hole, rather than using many line segments to form a curved line as with some wireframe models. It is also possible to "fair" or smooth one surface into another surface to provide a sculpted shape. Figure 4.4a shows the simple object with hidden lines removed

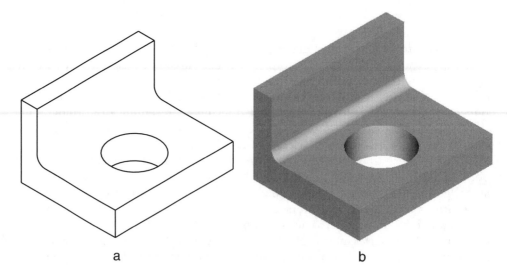

Figure 4.4
(a) 3-D wireframe model
with hidden lines removed.
(b) 3-D model with shading.

a   b

altogether. Although a surface model can be displayed to look like a wireframe, either with or without hidden lines, it can also be displayed by assigning different degrees of shading to the surfaces. A virtual light source is assumed to be near the object to provide a three-dimensional lighting effect as shown in Figure 4.4b. This is known as *shading* or *rendering*. Although a variety of shading techniques are available, all depend on determining how much light from a virtual light source strikes each portion of the virtual object. The use of shading provides a very realistic image of the object, which permits a much more vivid communication of the nature of the object. However, the problem that remains with a surface model is that the interior of the object remains undefined. The surface model just represents the shell of the object.

4.2 CAD AND SOLID MODELING

Solid modeling, the current state of the art in CAD, is the most sophisticated method of representing an object. Unlike wireframe or surface models, a solid model represents an object in the virtual environment just as it exists in reality, having volume as well as surfaces and edges. In this way, the interior of the object is represented in the model, as well as the outer surfaces.

The first attempt at solid modeling was a technique known as *constructive solid geometry* or *primitive modeling*, which is based on the combination of geometric primitives such as right rectangular prisms (blocks), right triangular prisms (wedges), spheres, cones, and cylinders. Each primitive could be scaled to the desired size, translated to the desired position, and rotated to the desired orientation. Then one primitive could be added to or subtracted from other primitives to make up a complex object. It is easy to see how two blocks plus a negative cylinder (hole), as shown in Figure 4.5, could represent an object similar to the one shown in Figure 4.4. (The rounded surface, or fillet, at the corner between the horizontal and vertical surfaces has been omitted.) The problem with constructive solid geometry is that the mental process of creating a solid model based on geometric primitives is much more abstract than the mental processes required for designing real-world objects.

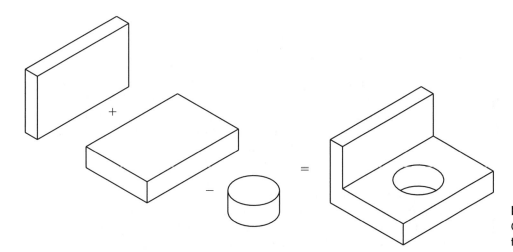

Figure 4.5
Combining geometric primitives to represent an object.

Constraint-based solid modeling overcomes the weakness of constructive solid geometry modeling by making the modeling process more intuitive. Instead of piecing together geometric primitives, the constraint-based modeling process begins with the creation of a 2-D sketch of the profile for the cross section of the part.

Here, "sketch" is the operative word. The sketch of the cross section begins much like the freehand sketch of the face of an object in an oblique projection. The only difference is that CAD software draws straight lines and perfect arcs. The initial sketch need not be particularly accurate; it need only reflect the basic geometry of the part's cross-sectional shape. Details of the cross section are added later. The next step is to constrain the 2-D sketch by adding enough dimensions and parameters to completely define the shape and size of the 2-D profile. The name ***constraint-based modeling*** arises because the shape of the initial 2-D sketch is "constrained" by adding dimensions to the sketch. Finally, a three-dimensional object is created by ***revolving*** or ***extruding*** the 2-D sketched profile. Figure 4.6 shows the result of revolving a simple L-shaped cross section by 270° about an axis and extruding the same L-shaped cross section along an axis. In either case, these solid bodies form the basic geometric solid shapes of the part. Other features can be subsequently added to modify the basic solid shape.

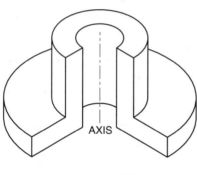

Revolved by 270°

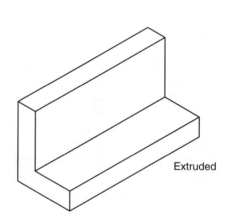

Extruded

Figure 4.6
Revolving by 270° and extruding an L-shaped cross section.

Professional Success

How Solid Models Are Used

Solid models are useful for purposes other than visualization. The solid model contains a complete mathematical representation of the object, inside and out. This mathematical representation is easily converted into specialized computer code that can be used for stress analysis, heat transfer analysis, fluid flow analysis, and computer-aided manufacturing.

Finite-element analysis (FEA) is a method used to subdivide the object under study into many small, simply shaped elements. The simple geometry of the finite elements allows the relatively simple application of the appropriate equations for the stress and deformation of the elements or for the heat transfer between elements. By properly relating nearby elements to one another, all of these equations for each element can be solved simultaneously. The final result is the stress, deformation (strain), or temperature throughout the object for a given applied load or thermal condition. The stress, deformation, or temperature is often displayed as a color map on the solid model, visually indicating the regions of high stress or temperature. From these results, the engineer can redesign the object to avoid stress concentrations, large deformations, or undesirable temperatures. Likewise, the fluid flow through or around an object can be calculated by applying similar FEA techniques using the equations of fluid flow to the regions bounded by the object. These analysis tools have greatly improved the design of many products.

Solid models can also be used in the manufacturing process. Software is available to automatically generate machine tool paths to machine the object on the basis of the solid model. The software simulates the removal of material from an initial block of material. This allows the engineer to optimize the machining operation. These tool paths can be downloaded onto computer numerical control (CNC) machine tools. The CNC machine tool automatically removes the desired surfaces from a block of material with high precision, allowing many identical parts to be machined automatically directly on the basis of the solid model. Alternatively, the solid model can be downloaded onto a rapid prototyping machine. This machine automatically builds up a part by driving lasers that solidify liquid plastic resin, a robotic system to dispense a fine bead of molten plastic, or a laser that cuts layers of paper. New systems are even available to build up metal parts in similar ways. In all these cases, layers are built up to become a physical model of the computer solid model, often within just a few hours. These manufacturing tools have made it possible to obtain parts from CAD models in several hours instead of several weeks.

Once the solid model is generated, all of the surfaces are automatically defined, so it is possible to shade it in the same way as a surface model is shaded. It is also easy to generate 2-D orthographic views of the object. This is a major advancement from other modeling schemes. With solid modeling, the two-dimensional drawings are produced as views of the three-dimensional virtual model of the object. In traditional CAD, the three-dimensional model is derived from the two-dimensional drawings. One might look at solid modeling as the sculpting of a virtual solid volume of material. Because the volume of the object is properly represented in a solid model, it is possible to slice through the object and show a view of the object that displays the interior detail. Once several solid objects have been created, they can be assembled in a virtual environment to ensure that they fit together properly and to visualize the assembled product.

4.3 THE NATURE OF SOLID MODELING

Solid modeling grew steadily in the 1980s, but it was not until Pro/ENGINEER® was introduced in 1988 and SolidWorks® was introduced in 1995 that solid modeling delivered on its promised gains in productivity. These gains result from five characteristics of the software: feature-based, constraint-based, parametric, history-based, and associative modeling.

Feature-based modeling attempts to make the modeling process more efficient by creating and modifying geometric ***features*** of a solid model in a way that represents how geometries are created using common manufacturing processes. Features in a part have a direct analogy to geometries that can be manufactured or machined. A ***base feature*** is a solid model that is roughly the size and shape of the part that is to be modeled. The base feature is the 3-D solid created by revolving or extruding a cross section, such as those shown in Figure 4.6. It can be thought of as the initial work block. All subsequent features reference the base feature either directly or indirectly. Additional features shape or refine the base feature. Examples of additional features include holes or cuts in the initial work block.

The analogy between feature-based modeling and common manufacturing processes is demonstrated in Figure 4.7 for making a handle for a pizza cutter. Beginning at the top of the figure, we follow the steps that an engineer would use to create a solid model, or virtual part, on the left and the steps that a machinist would take to create the same physical part in a machine shop on the right. The engineer, using solid modeling software, begins by creating a two-dimensional profile, or ***cross section***, of a part, in this case a circle (shown in isometric projection). The analogous step by a machinist is to choose a circular bar stock of material with the correct diameter. Next the engineer ***extrudes***, or stretches, the circular cross section along the axis perpendicular to the plane of the circle to create a three-dimensional base feature (a cylinder in this case). The equivalent action by a machinist is to cut off a length of bar stock to create an initial work block. Now the engineer adds features by cutting away material on the left end to reduce the diameter and by rounding the right end of the cylinder. The machinist performs similar operations on a lathe to remove material from the cylinder. Next the engineer creates a circular cut to form a hole through the cylinder on the right end. The machinist drills a hole in the right end of the cylinder. Finally, the engineer creates a pattern of groove cuts around the handle. Likewise the machinist cuts a series of grooves using a lathe. In similar fashion, a geometric shape could be added to the base feature in the solid model, analogous to a machinist welding a piece of metal to the work block. Feature-based techniques give the engineer the ability to easily create and modify common manufactured features. As a result, planning the manufacture of a part is facilitated by the correspondence between the features and the processes required to make them.

Constraint-based modeling permits the engineer or designer to incorporate "intelligence" into the design. Often this is referred to as ***design intent***. Unlike traditional CAD software, the initial sketch of a two-dimensional profile in constraint-based solid modeling does not need to be created with a great deal of accuracy. It just needs to represent the basic geometry of the cross section. The exact size and shape of the profile is defined through assigning enough parameters to fully "constrain" it. Some of this happens automatically within the software. For example, if two nearly parallel edges are within some preset tolerance range of parallel (say, 5 degrees), then the edges are automatically constrained to be parallel. As the part is resized, these edges will always remain parallel no matter what other changes are made. Likewise, if a hole is constrained to be at a certain distance from an edge, it will automatically remain at that distance from the edge, even if the edge is moved. This differs from traditional CAD, where both the hole and the edge would each be fixed at a particular coordinate location with respect to some arbitrary axes in space. If the edge were moved, the hole location would need to be respecified so that the hole remains the same distance from the edge. The advantage of constraint-based modeling is that the design intent of the engineer remains intact as the part is modified.

There are two primary types of constraints. ***Dimensional constraints*** are used to specify distances between items in a solid model. For example, a hole is prescribed by the location of its center, typically in terms of horizontal and vertical distances from features of a part such as edges or other holes. In addition, the

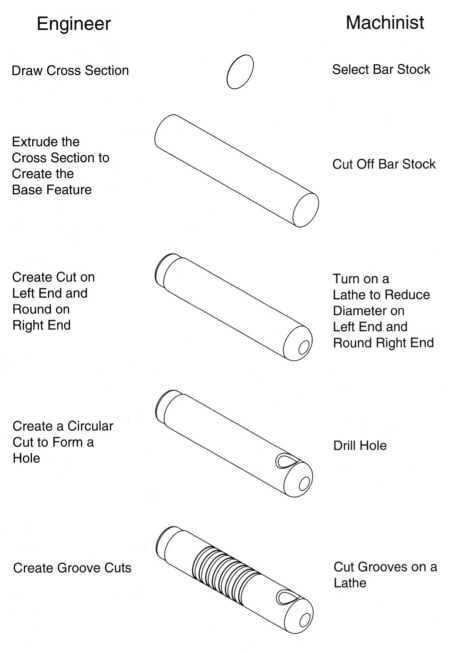

Engineer		Machinist
Draw Cross Section		Select Bar Stock
Extrude the Cross Section to Create the Base Feature		Cut Off Bar Stock
Create Cut on Left End and Round on Right End		Turn on a Lathe to Reduce Diameter on Left End and Round Right End
Create a Circular Cut to Form a Hole		Drill Hole
Create Groove Cuts		Cut Grooves on a Lathe

Figure 4.7
The analogy between feature-based modeling done by an engineer or designer and common manufacturing processes done by a machinist.

radius and depth of the hole need to be specified. Given these four dimensional constraints, the hole size, depth, and location are fully defined. There are other ways to use dimensional constraints to create a hole. Although it would be cumbersome in most cases, a hole could be specified by the location of three points on the circle forming the circumference of the hole plus a depth. Again, dimensional constraints (the locations of the three points on the circumference of the hole and the depth of the hole) define the hole.

Instead of specifying numerical dimensions, *geometric constraints* define positional relationships between entities in the model in terms of the geometry. For instance, a pipe can be formed from a solid circular rod by creating a hole that is concentric with the circumference of the rod. The radius and depth of the hole require dimensional constraints, but the position of the hole does not. Instead, the position can be prescribed purely by a geometric constraint, specifically that the hole is concentric with the rod. Examples of geometric constraints include tangency, parallelism, symmetry, concentricity, and so on. Typically, a combination of dimensional constraints and geometric constraints are used to fully "constrain" a part. Often geometric constraints are particularly useful in creating assemblies of individual parts, as demonstrated in Section 4.5.

Another aspect of solid modeling is that the model is **_parametric_**. This means that parameters of the model may be modified to change the geometry of the model. A dimension is a simple example of a parameter. When a dimension is changed, the geometry of the part is updated. Thus, the _parameter drives the geometry_. This is in contrast to other modeling systems, in which the geometry is changed, say, by stretching a part, and the dimension updates itself to reflect the stretched part. An additional feature of parametric modeling is that parameters can reference other parameters through relations or equations. For example, the position of the hole in Figure 4.4 could be specified with numerical values, say, 40 mm from the right side of the part. Or the position of the hole could be specified parametrically, so that the center of the hole is located at a position that is one-half of the total length of the part. If the total length was specified as 80 mm, then the hole would be 40 mm from either side. However, if the length was changed to 100 mm, then the hole would automatically be positioned at half of this distance, or 50 mm from either side. Thus, no matter what the length of the part is, the hole stays in the middle of the part. The power of this approach is that when one dimension is modified, all linked dimensions are updated according to specified mathematical relations, instead of having to update all related dimensions individually.

The last aspect of solid modeling is that the order in which parts are created is critical. This is known as **_history-based modeling_**. For example, a hole cannot be created before a solid volume of material in which the hole occurs has been modeled. If the solid volume is deleted, then the hole is deleted with it. This is known as a **_parent–child relation_**. The child (hole) cannot exist without the parent (solid volume) existing first. Parent–child relations are critical to maintaining design intent in a part. Most solid modeling software recognizes that if you delete a feature with a hole in it, you do not want the hole to remain floating around without being attached to a feature. Consequently, careful thought and planning of the base feature and initial additional features can have a significant effect on the ease of adding subsequent features and making modifications.

The **_associative_** character of solid modeling software causes modifications in one object to "ripple through" all associated objects. For instance, suppose that you change the diameter of a hole on the engineering drawing that was created based on your original solid model. The diameter of the hole will be automatically changed in the solid model of the part, too. In addition, the diameter of the hole will be updated on any assembly that includes that part. Similarly, changing the dimension in the part model will automatically result in updated values of that dimension in the drawing or assembly incorporating the part. This aspect of solid modeling software makes the modification of parts much easier and less prone to error.

As a result of being feature based, constraint based, parametric, history based, and associative, modern solid modeling software captures "design intent," not just the design. This comes about because solid modeling software incorporates engineering knowledge into the solid model with features, constraints, and relationships that preserve the intended geometric relationships in the model.

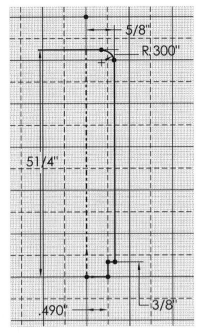

Figure 4.8
Sketch of the basic shape of the handle that will be revolved about the vertical, long-dash, short-dash centerline to create the base feature.

4.4 MODELING A PART IN CAD

The key characteristics of solid modeling can be most easily demonstrated by following the process to model a part in CAD. Consider modeling a pizza cutter handle. In this case, the part is modeled using SolidWorks, but other solid modeling software packages have similar capabilities. The designer or engineer starts with a cross section of the approximate shape of the handle that will be revolved, as shown in Figure 4.8. This is different from the process outlined in Figure 4.7, where the model starts with extruding a circular two-dimensional profile. Often there are several different approaches for modeling a particular part. Which is the best approach? The answer to this question depends on the skill of the CAD user, the complexity of the part, the potential for redesign, the design intent, and the preferences of the user. Unskilled users may prefer to "carve up" a solid block of material, like the approach shown in Figure 4.7. Skilled CAD users may extrude or revolve a cross section that already includes many of the features of the part. In Figure 4.8, the initial cross section includes the rounding on the top end and the reduced cross section on the bottom end. The designer begins by sketching lines from corner to corner. Because of the constraint-based nature of the CAD software, lines automatically snap to horizontal or vertical, even if the user does not draw them perfectly horizontal or vertical. After sketching the shape, the dimensions of the parts are specified. For instance, the handle is $5\frac{1}{4}$ inches long and will have a diameter of $1\frac{1}{4}$ inches after revolving the $\frac{5}{8}$-inch section about the ***centerline***, which is the vertical long-dash, short-dash line to the right of the $5\frac{1}{4}$-inch dimension. Although the dimensions are indicated in this cross section, solid modeling CAD software permits any of the dimensions to be changed later in the design process. After drawing the basic shape with sharp corners, a ***round***, or ***fillet***, is added to the upper right corner to round it off.

   Rotating this section about the centerline creates the basic shape of the handle, shown in Figure 4.9 as a shaded view. This is the base feature of the handle to which other features will be added. The first feature to be added is the

Figure 4.9
Handle base feature after revolving the shape shown in Figure 4.8 about the vertical centerline.

Figure 4.10
The first groove is cut by revolving a small cut around the circumference of the handle.

Figure 4.11
The handle grooves are created by patterning seven additional revolve cuts after the original cut.

groove pattern. This is done as two steps. First, a single groove is added by revolving a *cut* around the circumference of the handle, as shown in Figure 4.10 in a view that shows hidden lines in gray. Once a single feature has been created, it can be repeated by creating a *pattern* of identical features at a specified spacing. In Figure 4.11, the groove cut has been repeated seven more times to create an easily gripped handle. An advantage of feature-based modeling is that the size or shape of the cut used for the first groove can be changed later and that change will be propagated to the other groove cuts automatically.

The next feature that is added is the slot at the lower end of the handle. In adding any feature, a sketch is first created of the cross section of the feature. In Figure 4.12, a narrow rectangle is sketched on the bottom end of the handle and then dimensioned to define its size and position. To create the feature, this rectangular cross section is extruded as a cut into the handle to form the slot shown in Figure 4.13. The hole at the top of the handle begins with a sketch of a circle, shown

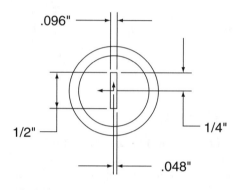

Figure 4.12
The rectangular slot is sketched on the bottom end of the handle and dimensioned.

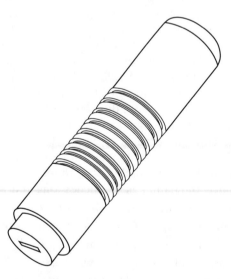

Figure 4.13
The rectangular cross section is extruded as a cut into the bottom of the handle to form a slot.

in Figure 4.14. The circle is extruded as a cut through the handle to form the hole, as shown in Figure 4.15. This figure is shown with the hidden lines in gray. This provides much of the detail of the handle, particularly the rectangular slot at the bottom of the handle, but the many lines forming the grooves are somewhat confusing compared with Figure 4.13, where the hidden lines have been removed. The only features remaining are the rounded edges of the hole and at the bottom of the handle. These have been added in Figure 4.16, which shows the completed handle.

The feature-based structure is evident in the design tree shown in Figure 4.17. The design tree is automatically created in the CAD software (in this case, Solid-Works) as the model is built, reflecting the features as they are added to the part. This is the history-based modeling aspect of solid modeling. At the top of the tree are three planes (**Front**, **Top**, **Right**) and the **Origin**, which together initially orient the object in space. **Revolve1** refers to the base feature shown in Figure 4.9, which is obtained from revolving the cross section shown in Figure 4.8 around a centerline. **Cut-Revolve1** refers to the first groove, which is cut around the circumference of the handle. **Axis3** is the line along which the groove is repeated to form the pattern **LPattern6**. There is a parent–child relation between the first groove and the subsequent grooves. The additional grooves cannot exist without the first groove, after which the subsequent grooves are patterned. **Cut-Extrude1** is the slot cut at the bottom of the handle, and **Cut-Extrude2** is the hole cut at the top of the handle. Finally, **Fillet1**, **Fillet2**, and **Fillet3** refer to the rounded edges of the hole and the two edges near the bottom of the handle. Because of the feature-based nature of solid modeling, it is quite easy to make modifications in the design. For instance, the diameter of the hole can be changed by simply clicking on **Cut-Extrude2** in the design tree and changing the dimension of the hole. This ability to easily modify individual features without affecting the rest of the part is one of the strengths of feature-based modeling.

The power of solid modeling is further demonstrated by making an even more sophisticated part. Figure 4.18 shows two halves of an injected molded version of the handle that are held together with four screws. Plastic injection molding

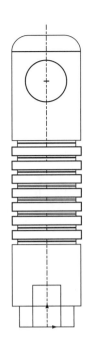

Figure 4.14
The circular hole at the top of the handle is sketched.

Figure 4.15
The circle is extruded as a cut through the top of the handle to create a hole. Note that the hidden lines of the rectangular slot are visible at the bottom of the handle.

Figure 4.16
The completed handle after rounding the sharp edges of the hole and at the bottom of the handle.

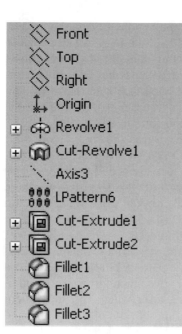

Figure 4.17

The individual features of the handle are shown in the design tree, reflecting how the part was created.

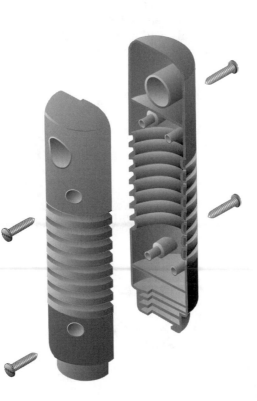

Figure 4.18

A more sophisticated version of the handle having thin walls suitable for injection molding.

permits the fabrication of complex parts at low cost. Solid plastic pellets are heated, and the molten plastic is injected at high pressure into a metal mold. After the plastic solidifies in the mold cavity, the two halves of the mold are separated and the part is ejected. Usually, injection-molded parts have thin walls to reduce the amount of plastic that is used in order to reduce the material costs and to allow uniform solidification of the molten plastic, which leads to a stronger part with few cosmetic and structural defects. Solid modeling makes the design of this part quite easy. First, the handle of Figure 4.16 is sliced in half by extruding a cut along the length of the handle, leaving only the portion shown in Figure 4.19. Next, four holes are added for the screws, as shown in Figure 4.20. Finally, the solid half of the handle is **shelled** to make all of the walls a uniform thickness. Ribs are added for structural strength, resulting in the part shown in Figure 4.18.

A powerful aspect of solid modeling is the ability to create smoothly contoured features called **lofts** or **blends** that enhance the style or ergonomics of a part. An example is the stylish, contoured handle shown in Figure 4.21. This version of the handle started out as a rounded rectangle on the left and an ellipse on the right, as shown in Figure 4.22. The line connecting the uppermost points of the rounded rectangle and the ellipse is straight, while the line connecting the

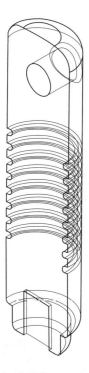

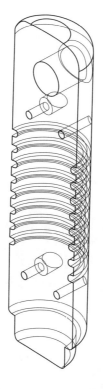

Figure 4.19
Extruding a cut to remove one-half of the handle leaves only the other half.

Figure 4.20
Holes are added for the screws. Shelling the solid half shown in this figure to create a uniform thin wall and adding ribs for strength results in the injection-molded version of the handle, shown in Figure 4.18.

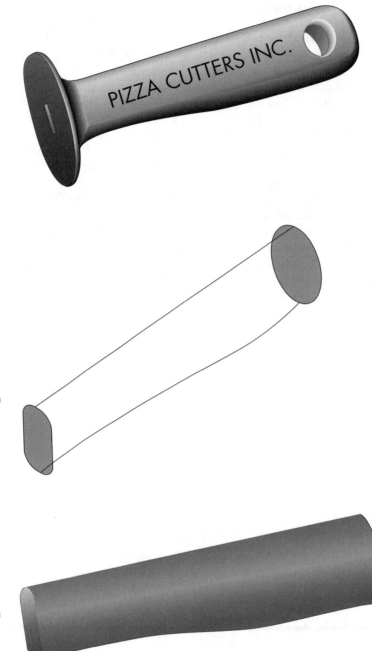

Figure 4.21
A more ergonomic version of the handle incorporating curved features called lofts or blends.

Figure 4.22
The handle shown in Figure 4.21 starts as rectangle with rounded corners on the left and an ellipse on the right, connected by a straight line on top and a gently curved line on the bottom.

Figure 4.23
After creating a loft between the rounded rectangle and ellipse in Figure 4.22, the contoured handle emerges.

lowermost points is gently curved. When the loft feature is implemented, the result is the smoothly contoured base feature, shown in Figure 4.23. Then other features can be added to the base feature, including the large diameter and the rectangular slot at the left end, the engraved lettering on the side, and the hole and rounded portion at the right end. Of course, the details of how specific features are implemented vary depending on the CAD software that is used. In the case of this handle, SolidWorks was used, but other CAD software programs have similar capabilities.

4.5 VIRTUAL ASSEMBLY OF PARTS

One of the great advantages of solid modeling software is that it allows engineers or designers to assemble modeled parts to create a virtual assembly. This helps the designer to work out problems with part interactions early in the design phase, before manufacturing has begun. Often it is possible to check automatically for clearances or interferences between parts. A virtual assembly also permits the engineer or designer to get an idea of what the assembled product looks like before it is fabricated.

In the case of the pizza cutter, the assembly begins by bringing two parts of the pizza cutter into the assembly window of the CAD software, in this case the rivet and one arm, as shown in Figure 4.24. Geometric constraints are used to orient the two parts properly. For example, a geometric constraint is used to make the shaft of the rivet and the cylindrical surface of the hole concentric with one another, as shown in Figure 4.25. Next, the surface of the arm that the arrow points to in Figure

Figure 4.24
The pizza cutter assembly begins as two parts, the rivet and an arm, oriented randomly in space.

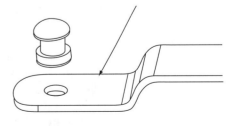

Figure 4.25
The shaft of the rivet is constrained to be concentric with the hole in the arm.

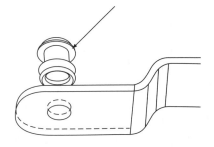

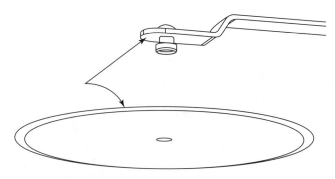

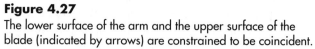

Figure 4.26
The underside of the head of the rivet (see arrow) is constrained to be coincident with the upper plane of the arm (indicated by the arrow in Figure 4.25).

Figure 4.27
The lower surface of the arm and the upper surface of the blade (indicated by arrows) are constrained to be coincident.

4.25 must be constrained so that it coincides with the underside of the head of the rivet that the surface the arrow points to in Figure 4.26. The blade can be added by making the hole in the blade concentric with the shaft of the rivet and by making the two surfaces with arrows in Figure 4.27 coincident. Likewise, the hole in the second arm is concentric to the shaft of the rivet, and the surfaces indicated in Figure 4.28 are made coincident. At this point, the two arms can still rotate with respect to one another; hence, a geometric constraint is added so that the surfaces indicated in Figure 4.29 are parallel. Similar geometric constraints can be used to assemble the remaining parts to create the finished assembly, shown in Figure 4.30.

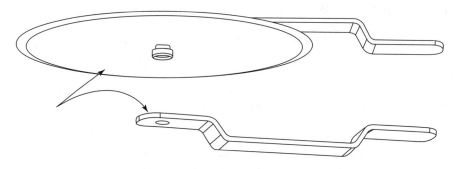

Figure 4.28
The lower surface of the blade and the upper surface of the second arm (indicated by arrows) are constrained to be coincident.

Once the pizza cutter is assembled, it is possible to check for ***interference*** between parts. In this case, there was an error in the metal guard that is at the end of the handle to prevent the user's hand from slipping down the handle onto the sharp blade. Notice in Figure 4.31 that the rectangular assembly that holds the blade cannot fit through the circular hole in the guard. The solid modeling software will detect this problem, which can be fixed by returning to the CAD file of the guard and changing the hole feature from a circular hole to a rectangular hole. Because of the associative nature of the CAD software, this modification in the part will be automatically reflected in the assembly, resulting in the modified guard in Figure 4.32, shown in an exploded view.

The steps that have been shown in creating the handle and the pizza cutter assembly are merely examples of how solid-modeling CAD software can be used in the design of parts. There are many alternative methods of accomplishing the same thing, such as changing the order in which the features are added to the base feature

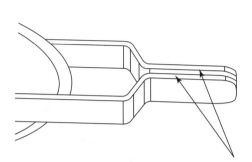

Figure 4.29
The sides of the two arms (indicated by arrows) are constrained to be parallel so that the arms are aligned with each other.

Figure 4.30
The assembled pizza cutter.

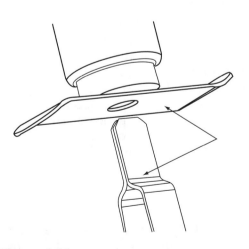

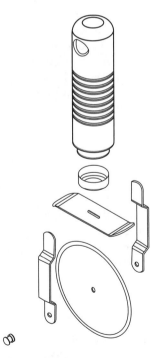

Figure 4.31
The rectangular ends of the arms cannot fit through the circular hole of the guard, a problem that is automatically detected by the CAD software as interference between the parts.

Figure 4.32
An exploded view of the pizza cutter showing the guard with a rectangular hole instead of a circular hole.

or changing the order in which the parts are assembled. Furthermore, many details have been left out, particularly with regard to differences in how various CAD software packages accomplish the creation of parts and assemblies. However, the steps used to create the handle and the pizza cutter assembly demonstrate some key characteristics of solid modeling: starting with a base feature and adding other features to it; using constraints, both dimensional and geometric, to incorporate "design intent"; and using the associative capability of the software to permit changes to ripple through associated objects such as the assembly.

Professional Success

File Transfer Between CAD Systems

As the engineering world becomes more interconnected with e-mail and the Internet, engineering graphics are routinely transferred as electronic documents both within and outside of a company. Sometimes this involves the need to import or export drawings created using one CAD system to another CAD system. Each CAD system usually saves a part's geometry and feature-based design intent in its own format. Several standard formats exist that can be used to transfer documents between different CAD programs. Translators are usually available within most CAD software to import and export data files that are in these standard formats. For instance, commonly used formats for 3-D solid modeling file exchange are the Initial Graphics Exchange Specification, or IGES, and Standardized Exchange of Product, or STEP. Typical two-dimensional CAD drawing formats include the DXF and DWG formats. However, a problem with several of these standard formats is that the design intent built into the model via feature-based modeling is often lost in the standard format. This makes it difficult to modify the solid model after it has been exported to a different CAD system. To solve this problem, software is now available to translate not only the geometry of the solid model, but also the full feature-based design intent between major CAD systems.

KEY TERMS

Associative modeling	Feature	Rendering
Base Feature	Feature-based modeling	Revolve
Centerline	Fillet	Round
Constraint-based modeling	Geometric constraint	Shading
	History-based modeling	Shelling
Constructive solid geometry	Interference	Solid modeling
	Loft	Surface model
Design intent	Parametric modeling	Sweep
Dimensional constraint	Parent–child relation	Wireframe model
Extrude	Primitive modeling	

PROBLEMS

4.1 The wireframe model shown in Figure 4.33 is a small cube centered within a large cube. The nearest corners of the two cubes are connected. For instance, the lower left front corners of both cubes are connected with a line. This wireframe model is ambiguous; that is, it could represent several different solid bodies. Freehand sketch or trace the figure. Then use dashed lines for hidden lines to show at least two different solid-model configurations that are possible for this wireframe model.

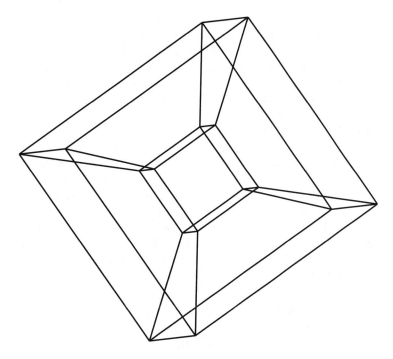

Figure 4.33

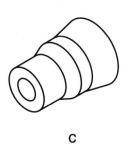

a

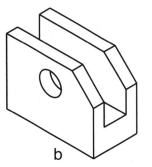

b

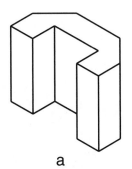

c

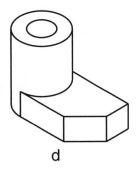

d

Figure 4.34

4.2 Using a technique similar to that shown in Figure 4.5, freehand sketch the geometric primitives that could be added or subtracted to form the objects shown in Figure 4.34. (The hole in Figure 4.34b is only through the face shown, not the back face. The holes in Figures 4.34c and 4.34d are through holes.)

4.3 Sketch the cross section that should be revolved to create the objects shown in Figure 4.35. Include in the sketch the axis about which the cross section is revolved.

4.4 Sketch at least two cross sections that could be extruded to form a base feature for the objects shown in Figure 4.36. Use cross sections that can be extruded into a base feature from which material is only removed, not added. Make sure that the cross sections that you propose minimize the number of additional features necessary to modify the base feature. (The hole in Figures 4.36a is only through the face shown, not the back face. The holes in Figures 4.36b, 4.36c, and 4.36e are through holes.)

4.5 Consider the following objects. Sketch what the base feature would look like. List what features would be added to model the object. The type of base feature to be used (extrude, revolve, or both) is noted.

(a) hexagonal cross section of a wooden pencil that is sharpened to a point (do not include eraser)—extrude.

(b) coffee mug without the handle—revolve.

(c) nail—extrude and revolve.

(d) push pin—revolve.

(e) baseball bat—revolve.

(f) broom handle—revolve and extrude.

(g) ceiling fan blade—extrude.

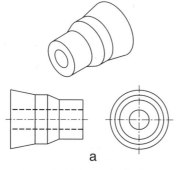

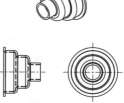

a

b

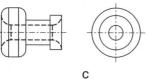

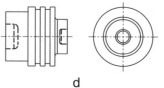

c

d

Figure 4.35

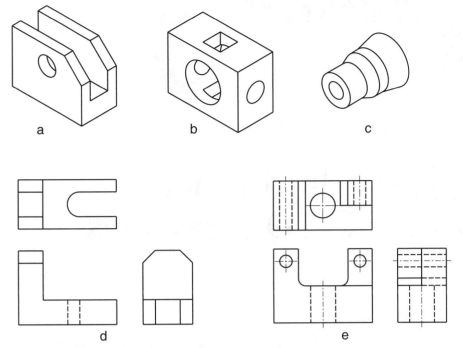

Figure 4.36

(h) cinder block—extrude.

(i) compact disk—revolve and extrude.

(j) single staple (before being deformed)—extrude.

(k) automobile tire—revolve.

(l) gear—extrude.

(m) round toothpick—revolve.

4.6 Describe parametric modeling and give an example of a family of parts where parametric modeling would be useful.

4.7 Describe constraint-based modeling and explain how it relates to design intent. Note the difference between dimensional constraints and geometric constraints.

4.8 The example of modeling a pizza cutter handle shown in Figure 4.16 began with the sketch shown in Figure 4.8. Then grooves were added and edges were rounded at the bottom of the handle. Sketch the shape that could be revolved to form a base feature that already includes the grooves and rounded edges.

4.9 The example of solid modeling a pizza cutter handle shown in Figure 4.16 began with the sketch shown in Figure 4.8. Instead, assume that the initial sketch that is revolved to create the base feature is simply a rectangle with a horizontal dimension of $\frac{5}{8}$ inch and a vertical dimension of $5\frac{1}{4}$ inches. List the additional features that would be added to the base feature to create the handle shown in Figure 4.16.

Standard Practice for CAD Drawings

Objectives

After reading this chapter, you should be able to

- Explain why drawing standards are used
- Choose the proper sheet layout
- Read and understand the scale of a drawing
- Differentiate different linetypes used in engineering drawings
- Properly place dimensions on a drawing
- Read and understand section, auxiliary, and detail views on a drawing
- Read and understand screw thread designations on a drawing
- Read an assembly drawing

OVERVIEW

Drawing standards and conventions are used to clarify engineering drawings and simplify their creation. For example, standard sizes for drawings are used, and standard types and weights of lines designate different items on a drawing. Although CAD software automates most aspects of a drawing, many decisions are still up to the user. For example, the proper placement of dimensions on drawings is helpful in making the drawing more readable. In addition, internal or small details of the part can be displayed using special views. Screw threads are too detailed to be clear on most drawings, so standard representations are used for screw threads.

5.1 INTRODUCTION TO DRAWING STANDARDS

Not only is the accurate and clear depiction of details of a part necessary in an engineering drawing, but it is also necessary that the drawing conform to commonly accepted standards or conventions. There are two reasons for the existence of standards and conventions. First, using standard symbols and projections ensures a clear interpretation of the drawing by the viewer. An example of the problem of differing presentations is the use of the third-angle orthographic projection in North America and the first-angle orthographic projection elsewhere in the world. (The top and bottom views and the right and left views are reversed in third-angle and first-angle projections.) This can bring about confusion if, for example, a U. S. engineer tries to interpret a German drawing. A second reason for using conventions is to simplify the task of creating engineering drawings. For example, the symbol Ø associated with a dimension indicates that the dimension is a diameter of a circular feature. Without this convention, it would be more difficult to unambiguously represent diameter dimensions on a drawing.

Most CAD programs automatically use a standardized presentation of drawings, usually based on standards from the American National Standards Institute (ANSI; see www.ansi.org) in the United States and the International

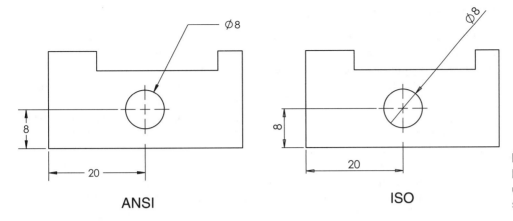

Figure 5.1
Drawings of the same object using the ANSI and ISO standards.

Standards Organization (ISO; see www.iso.org) in the rest of the world. Other standards that are often included as options in CAD software include BSI (British Standards Institution), DIN (Deutsches Institut für Normung, or German Institute for Standardization), GB (Guojia Biaozhun, Chinese standards), GOST (standards for the Commonwealth of Independent States of the former Soviet Union), and JIS (Japanese Industrial Standards). The differences between the commonly used standards are relatively minor, and are typically related to symbols that are used and the details of how dimensions or other items appear on a drawing. For example, Figure 5.1 shows the dimensions of a part in one view using both the ANSI and ISO standards. Notice that the numbers for the dimensions in the ANSI standard are *unidirectional*, having the same orientation, whereas the values for the dimensions in the ISO drawing are *aligned* with the dimension line. Although the ISO standard may seem a bit harder to read, particularly for someone who usually uses the ANSI standard, both standards convey the same information. The BSI, DIN, GB, GOST, and JIS drawings look identical to the ISO drawing shown in Figure 5.1, although other minor details not shown in this drawing may differ.

Even with the use of CAD software to ensure standard presentation in drawings, it is up to the engineer to implement drawing standards in some cases. An example is in the placement of dimensions in a drawing. The user controls where dimensions appear on the drawing. Furthermore, even in cases where the CAD software automatically implements drawing standards, it is still necessary to understand what the conventions mean so that they are properly interpreted.

There is some variability among different CAD software packages in how various details are shown. For instance, the length of centerlines, the type of line used for hidden lines, and the shape of arrowheads may differ from one CAD software package to another. An example is the gray color sometimes used for hidden lines. Although hidden lines are generally shown as dashed lines in final drawings, they may be shown as gray or other colors while the part is being modeled. Another example is the length of the lines forming the cross at the center of the circle in Figure 5.1. These lines should normally be quite short to form a small cross, as shown in the figure. However, the length of these lines depends on settings in the software. If the user does not adjust the settings properly, the lines can be much longer or shorter. In most cases these variations are not significant. However, in this book, examples are shown that were created using different standard CAD packages, so they may differ slightly from one another in terms of these details.

5.2 SHEET LAYOUTS

Engineering drawings are created on standard-size sheets that are designated by the code indicated in Table 5.1. The ISO drawing sizes are just slightly smaller than ANSI sizes. Engineering drawings are almost always done in "landscape" orientation so that the long side of the drawing is horizontal. The choice of drawing size depends upon the complexity of the object depicted in the drawing. The drawing should be sized so that the projections of the part, dimensions, and notes all fall within the borders of the drawing with adequate spacing, so that the drawing is not cluttered. The drawing should be large enough so that all details are readily evident and readable. As a result, regardless of the physical size of the part, simple parts are usually drawn on smaller sheets because it is not necessary to show much detail. Complex parts are usually drawn on larger sheets so that there is room to show adequate detail. When using CAD software, it is necessary to consider the printed drawing size in addition to the drawing size on the computer screen. On the computer screen, it is possible to zoom in to read detailed items, but this cannot be done for a printed drawing. Consequently, the sheet size should be chosen carefully.

Table 5.1 Standard Sheet Sizes.

ANSI	ISO
A—8.50″ × 11.00″	A4—210 mm × 297 mm
B—11.00″ × 17.00″	A3—297 mm × 420 mm
C—17.00″ × 22.00″	A2—420 mm × 594 mm
D—22.00″ × 34.00″	A1—594 mm × 841 mm
E—34.00″ × 44.00″	A0—841 mm × 1189 mm

The *title block* on a drawing records important information about the drawing. Normally the title block of a drawing is in the lower right corner of the drawing. ANSI standard title blocks can be used, but often individual companies use their own standard title block. The title block, such as the one shown in Figure 5.2, is used primarily for drawing control within a company. The title block includes information regarding the part depicted in the drawing, such as its name and part number; the person who created the drawing; persons who checked or approved the drawing; dates the drawing was created, revised, checked, and approved; the drawing number; and the name of the company. This information allows the company to track the drawing within the company if questions arise about the design.

Other information can appear in the title block to provide details about the manufacture of the part, such as the material for the part, the general tolerances, the

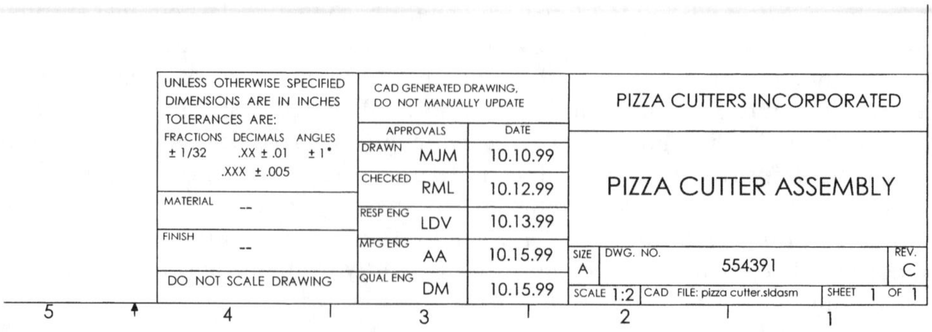

Figure 5.2
A typical title block.

UNLESS OTHERWISE SPECIFIED DIMENSIONS ARE IN INCHES TOLERANCES ARE:	CAD GENERATED DRAWING, DO NOT MANUALLY UPDATE		PIZZA CUTTERS INCORPORATED	
FRACTIONS DECIMALS ANGLES	APPROVALS	DATE		A
± 1/32 .XX ± .01 ± 1° .XXX ± .005	DRAWN MJM	10.10.99		
	CHECKED RML	10.12.99	PIZZA CUTTER ASSEMBLY	
MATERIAL --	RESP ENG LDV	10.13.99		
FINISH --	MFG ENG AA	10.15.99	SIZE	DWG. NO. 554391	REV.
			A		C
DO NOT SCALE DRAWING	QUAL ENG DM	10.15.99	SCALE 1:2	CAD FILE: pizza cutter.sldasm	SHEET 1 OF 1

5   4   3   2   1

surface finish specifications, and general instructions about manufacturing the part (such as "remove all burrs"). Many times, though, this information is shown as notes on the drawing rather than in the title block.

Finally the title block provides information about the drawing itself, such as the units used in dimensioning (typically inches or millimeters) and the scale of the drawing. The *scale* of the drawing indicates the ratio of the size on the drawing to the size of the actual object. It can be thought of as the degree to which the object is enlarged or shrunk in the drawing. Scales on drawings are denoted in several ways. For instance, consider an object that is represented in the drawing as half of its actual size. Then the drawing is created such that 1 inch on the drawing represents 2 inches on the physical object. This can be reported in the Scale box in the title block as HALF SCALE, HALF SIZE, 1 = 2, 1:2, or 1/2″ = 1″. In the numerical representations, the left number is the length on the drawing and the right number is the length of the actual object. A part that is drawn twice as large as its physical size would be denoted as DOUBLE, 2× (denoting "2 times"), 2 = 1, or 2:1. In some cases, such as architectural drawings, the scale can be quite large. For instance, 1/4″ = 1′–0″ corresponds to a scale of 1:48, where ″ denotes inches and ′ denotes feet. Common scales used in engineering drawing are 1 = 1, 1 = 2, 1 = 4, 1 = 8, and 1 = 10 for English units and 1:1, 1:2, 1:5, 1:10, 1:20, 1:50, and 1:100 for metric units. A 1:1 scale is often specified as FULL SCALE or FULL SIZE.

5.3 LINES

The types of lines used in engineering drawing are standardized. Different linetypes have different meanings, and understanding these different types of lines makes interpreting drawings easier. The linetypes vary in thickness and in the length and number of dashes in dashed lines. Most CAD software automatically produces linetypes that correspond to the way the line is used in the drawing. Figure 5.3 shows some of the more commonly used linetypes:

- *Visible lines* (thick, solid lines) represent the outline of the object that can be seen in the current view.
- *Hidden lines* (thin, dashed lines) represent features that are hidden behind surfaces in the current view.

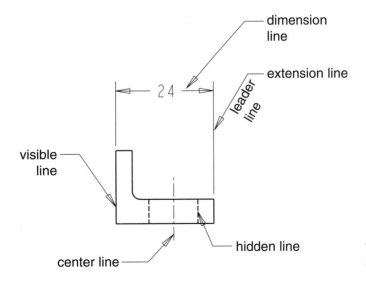

Figure 5.3
Types of lines used in drawings.

- *Centerlines* or *symmetry lines* (thin, long-dash/short-dash lines) mark axes of rotationally symmetric parts or features.
- *Dimension lines* (thin lines with arrowheads at each end) indicate sizes in the drawing.
- *Extension lines* or *witness lines* (thin lines) extend from the object to the dimension line to indicate which feature is associated with the dimension.
- *Leader lines* (thin, solid lines terminated with arrowheads) are used to indicate a feature with which a dimension or note is associated.

Other linetypes are used for break lines (lines with zigzags) that show where an object is "broken" in the drawing to save drawing space or reveal interior features and cutting plane lines (thick lines with double short dashes and perpendicular arrows at each end) that show the location of cutting planes for section views. The arrowheads for dimension lines, leader lines, and other types of lines may be filled or not filled, depending on the CAD software. Many engineering graphics textbooks prefer filled arrowheads.

It is common in technical drawings that two lines in a particular view coincide. When this occurs, a convention known as the *precedence of lines* dictates which line is shown: visible lines have precedence over hidden lines, which have precedence over centerlines. An example is shown in Figure 5.4. In the top view, line A is shown

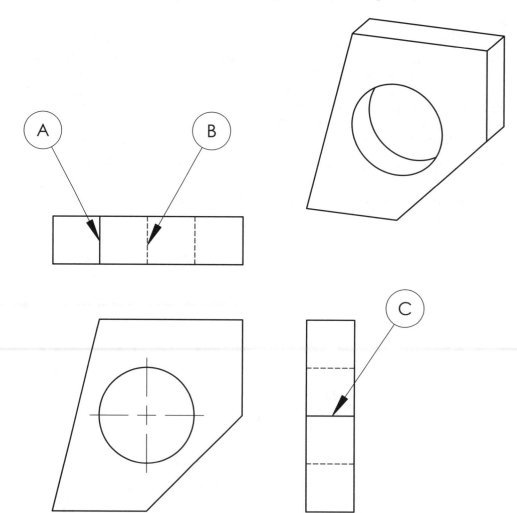

Figure 5.4

An example showing the precedence of lines.

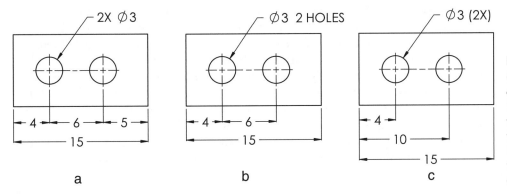

Figure 5.5

(a) An overdimensioned drawing; (b) A dimensioning scheme that emphasizes the 6-mm distance between the holes; (c) A dimensioning scheme that emphasizes the distance from the left edge to each hole.

as a solid visible line, since the visible line that forms the top left edge has precedence over the dashed hidden line for the side of the hole. Line B of the top view is shown as a dashed hidden line, since it has precedence over the centerline of the hole. Likewise, line C in the side view is shown as a visible line, since the edge on the right side has precedence over the centerline of the hole. Visible lines, hidden lines, and centerlines all have precedence over extension lines.

Conventions also exist for the intersection of lines in a drawing. For instance, an extension line is always drawn so that there is a slight, visible gap between its end and the outline of the object, as shown in Figure 5.3. Similarly, *center marks* appearing at the center of a circle are drawn so that the short dashes of each line intersect to form a small cross, as shown in Figure 5.5. Fortunately, CAD software automatically takes care of most of the details related to lines, as well as their length and position. The engineer or designer need only know how to properly interpret the various linetypes.

5.4 DIMENSION PLACEMENT AND CONVENTIONS

Engineering drawings are usually drawn to scale, but it is still necessary to specify numerical dimensions for convenience and to ensure accuracy. In general, sufficient dimensions must be provided to define the geometry of the part precisely, but redundant dimensions should be avoided. Furthermore, dimensions on the drawing should reflect the way the part is made or the critical dimensions of the part. For example, Figure 5.5 shows three drawings of a plate with two holes. Figure 5.5a is *overdimensioned*, having one redundant dimension. It is clear that, given the distances from the left edge to the left hole, the distance from the right edge to the right hole, and the overall width of the plate, the distance between the holes has to be 6 mm. Thus, the 6-mm dimension could be omitted. However, the dimensions that are shown in the drawing often suggest which dimensions are most important. If the 6-mm dimension in Figure 5.5a were omitted, it would suggest that the distance between each hole and the nearest edge of the plate is more important than the distance between the holes. But suppose, instead, that the distance between the holes is critical. This might be necessary if the holes in the plate are supposed to align with another part. Then the dimensions shown in Figure 5.5b would clearly indicate that the distance between the holes is the most important dimension by omitting the dimension from the right hole to the right edge. Figure 5.5c indicates that the distance from the left edge to each hole, not the distance between the holes, is critical. The engineer or designer must consider the optimal way to display dimensions to clearly convey which dimensions are most important.

The position of the dimensions is also important. Figure 5.6 shows several examples of incorrect ways of dimensioning a drawing. It is best to avoid having dimensions inside the boundary of the object, as is the case in Figure 5.6a. Dimensions should be kept outside the boundaries of the object whenever possible, unless clarity is improved in some way by having them inside the boundary. Dimension lines should not be too close to the boundaries of the object, as is the case with the 40-mm dimension in Figure 5.6b. A typical spacing is 10 mm ($\frac{3}{8}$ inch) for the distance of the first dimension from the object and 6 mm ($\frac{1}{4}$ inch) for the spacing between subsequent dimensions. It is also difficult to interpret the drawing when the dimension line coincides with a visible line of the object, as is the case in Figure 5.6b for the 20-mm

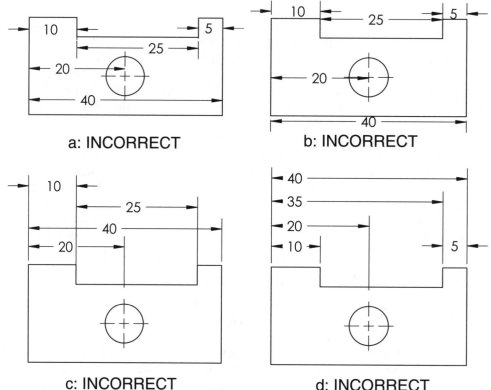

Figure 5.6
(a) Placing dimensions on the object is incorrect; (b) Placing dimensions so that dimension lines align with visible lines of the object or are very close to the object is incorrect; (c) Placing dimensions in random order is incorrect; (d) Overdimensioning is incorrect; (e) A properly dimensioned drawing.

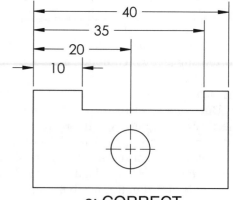

dimension (the dimension line coincides with the center mark line) and the 25-mm dimension (the dimension line looks like a continuation of the upper boundary of the part). In Figure 5.6c, the dimensions are in a random order with some smaller dimensions farther from the boundary of the object (such as the 10-mm dimension) than larger dimensions (such as the 40-mm dimension). This results in dimension lines crossing extension lines, which should be avoided. It is often helpful to stack the dimensions in order of increasing length as shown in Figure 5.6d. However, there are three problems in this case. First, placing the dimension numbers right above one another is somewhat difficult to read. Second, there is a redundant dimension—the 5-mm dimension is unnecessary. Third, the 10-mm dimension is so small that there is no dimension line, and only the arrowheads appear. This is readily corrected by placing the arrowheads outside of the extension lines instead of inside, as shown in Figure 5.6e. In addition, in this case the dimension numbers are staggered, or offset, by a small amount to make them more easily readable. All the dimensioning conventions are aimed at making the drawing as easily readable as possible so that the information on the drawing is conveyed clearly to the reader.

It is natural for a person reading the drawings to look for the dimensions of a feature in the view where the feature occurs in its most characteristic shape and where it is visible (as opposed to hidden). This is known as ***contour dimensioning***. For example, the location and size of a hole should be dimensioned in the view where the hole appears as a circle. Likewise, it is best to show the overall dimensions of the object in a view that is most descriptive of the object. If possible, both the horizontal and vertical location of a feature should be dimensioned in the same view. The upper part of Figure 5.7 shows an object properly dimensioned in millimeters to show the relation of the dimensions to the features in the most obvious manner. In the lower part of Figure 5.7, the dimensioning has several problems. The overall vertical dimensions of the L-shaped profile, the 8- and 35-mm dimensions, are shown on the right view where it is not clear that the object is L-shaped. The diameter of the hole is shown in a view where the hole is shown only as a pair of parallel hidden lines, not as a circle. And the vertical location of the hole is shown in one view, while the horizontal location is shown in another view. Finally, the vertical location of the hole is shown as a distance to its edge (the 7-mm dimension). Generally, the locations of holes should be dimensioned to the center of the hole.

The conventions for millimeter and inch dimensioning are different. For millimeter dimensioning, dimensions less than 1 mm have a zero preceding the decimal point, and integer dimensions may or may not include a decimal point and following zeros. Thus, legitimate millimeter dimensions are 0.8, 6, 8.00, and 1.5. Inch dimensions do not include a zero before the decimal point for values less than 1 inch. Zeros to the right of the decimal point are usually included. Legitimate inch dimensions are .800, 6.00, 8.00, and 1.500. For both millimeter and inch dimensions, the number of digits to the right of the decimal point may be used to indicate the tolerance (acceptable variation). It is standard practice to omit the units for dimensions. However, it is wise to note the units in the title block or as a note on the drawing.

Circles and arcs are dimensioned using special symbols and rules. A radius is denoted using a leader line with an arrow pointing at the arc, as shown in the upper portion of Figure 5.7. Sometimes a small cross is placed at the center of the radius. The position of the center should be dimensioned unless the radius is for a rounded edge, in which case the arc is positioned by virtue of being tangent at its ends to the sides forming the corner that is rounded, as shown in Figure 5.7. The dimension for a radius begins with a capital letter R to indicate radius. Full circles are dimensioned

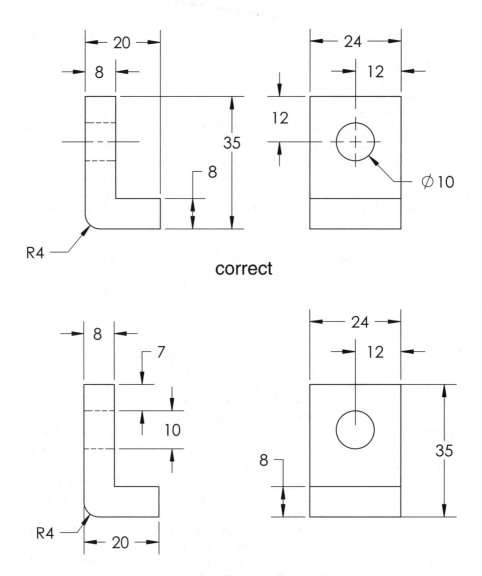

correct

poorly dimensioned

Figure 5.7
Properly and improperly dimensioned drawings.

using the diameter with a leader line having an arrow pointing at the circle, as shown in Figures 5.1 and 5.7. If space permits, the leader line can extend across a diameter of the circle with arrows at each end of the diameter. The dimension for a diameter begins with the Greek letter phi (∅) to indicate diameter. The location of the center of the circle must also be dimensioned.

Sometimes maintaining clarity makes it preferable to dimension several concentric circles from a side view, where the circle does not appear as a circle, thus violating the rule to dimension a feature in its most characteristic shape. This also permits the depth of the feature to be indicated along with the diameter in the same view of the object. Figure 5.8 shows how concentric circles can be dimensioned from a side view. The diameter dimensions to the left use ∅ to indicate diameter. The dimensions above the object indicate the length of the features corresponding to particular diameters along the axis.

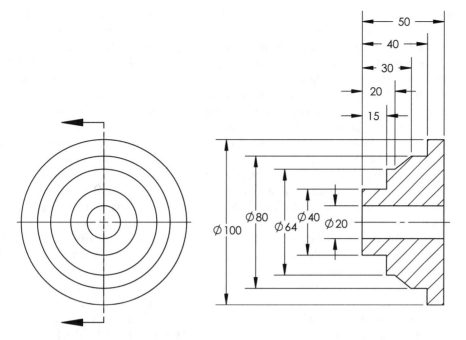

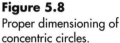

Figure 5.8
Proper dimensioning of
concentric circles.

Angles are dimensioned as decimals or in degrees and minutes (60 minutes is one degree), so that 32.5 and 32°30′ are equivalent, where ′ indicates minutes. The dimension line for an angle is drawn as an arc with its center at the apex of the angle, as shown in Figure 5.9a. Here a combination of angles and length dimensions are used to fully dimension the object. Note that the arrows are "inside" for the 76° dimension and "outside" for the 45° dimension. Either type can be used, depending on the space available and readability. Figure 5.9b shows how the same shape can be dimensioned without using any angles. In some ways, this figure is less clear than Figure 5.9a, because some extension lines cross and there are more dimension lines. At first glance, it may appear that Figure 5.9b is overdimensioned, since the 2-inch dimension on the top is simply the sum of the two 1-inch dimensions on the bottom. However, strictly speaking, all of these dimensions are necessary. If the lower right 1-inch dimension were omitted, the upper-right corner of the object would not

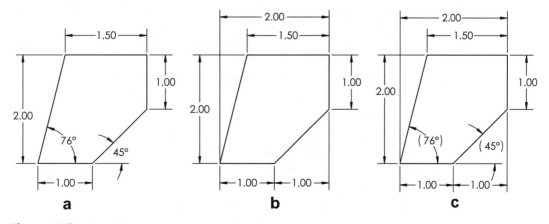

Figure 5.9
(a) Properly dimensioned object using angles; (b) Properly dimensioned object without using angles; (c) Angles are in parentheses to indicate that they are reference dimensions.

necessarily be constrained to be 90°. In practice, when lines are drawn at right angles, a 90° angle is usually implied, so the lower right 1-inch dimension could be omitted without creating any ambiguity. Figure 5.9c shows the length dimensions in addition to the angles. While this drawing is **overdimensioned**, the display of the angles may aid in clarifying the dimensions for the reader of the drawing. Whether to include extra dimensions depends on what critical aspects of the dimensions need to be indicated on the drawing. If it is necessary that the angle in Figure 5.9c be exactly 45°, then this angle should be specified on the drawing and the 1-inch horizontal dimension should be in parentheses to indicate it is a **reference dimension** provided for convenience to the reader. On the other hand, if the 1-inch dimension is critical, it should be indicated on the drawing and the angle could be provided as a reference dimension for convenience, as shown in Figure 5.9c. Reference dimensions are provided only for information to help in interpreting the drawing. They are not intended to be measured or to be used to govern the manufacture of the part. Generally, it is preferable to show the dimensions in the clearest form possible. For this object, Figure 5.9a is superior to the other dimensioning schemes by using the fewest dimensions that overlap the least.

Multiple features that are identical need not be individually dimensioned. For example, the diameter of the two 3-mm holes in Figure 5.5a are dimensioned with a leader line to one hole with the dimension 2 × Ø3. The 2× indicates "two times." Alternative dimensions are Ø3 (2×), Ø3 2 PLACES, or Ø3 2 HOLES.

There are several other "rules" for dimensioning:

- Dimension lines should be outside of the outline of a part whenever possible.

- Dimension lines should not cross one another.

- Dimensions should be indicated on a view that shows the true length of the feature. This is particularly important when dimensioning features that are on a surface that is at an angle to the plane of the orthographic view.

- Each feature should be dimensioned only once. Do not duplicate the same dimension in different views.

- Dimension lines should be aligned and grouped when possible to promote clarity and uniform appearance. See, for example, the placement of the horizontal dimensions in Figure 5.6e.

- The numerical dimension and arrows should be placed between the extension lines where space permits. If there is space only for the dimension, but not the arrows, place the arrows outside of the extension lines. When the space is too small for either the arrows or the numerical value, place both outside of the extension lines. See Figure 5.7 for examples.

- Place the dimension no closer than about 10 mm ($\frac{3}{8}$ inch) from the object's outline.

- Dimensions should be placed in clear spaces, as close as possible to the feature they describe.

- When dimensions are nested (such as the horizontal dimensions in Figure 5.6e), the smallest dimensions should be closest to the object.

- Avoid crowding dimensions. Leave at least 6 mm ($\frac{1}{4}$ inch) between parallel dimension lines.

- Extension lines may cross visible lines of the object.

- Dimensions that apply to two adjacent views should be placed between the views, unless clarity is enhanced by placing them elsewhere. The dimension should be attached to only one view. Extension lines should not connect two views.

- Dimension lines and extension lines should not cross, if possible. Extension lines may cross other extension lines.

- A centerline may be extended to serve as an extension line, in which case it is still drawn as a centerline.

- Centerlines should not extend from one view to another view.

- Leader lines are usually sloped at about 30°, 45°, or 60° and are never horizontal or vertical.

- Numerical values for dimensions should be approximately centered between arrowheads unless several dimensions are nested, as in Figure 5.6e. In this case, dimensions should be staggered.

- When a rough, noncritical dimension (such as a round) is indicated on a drawing, add the note TYP to the dimension to indicate that the dimension is "typical" or approximate.

- Sometimes it is helpful to include a ***reference dimension*** that is redundant or otherwise unnecessary, but is included for the convenience of the person reading the drawing. Such dimensions are usually in parentheses.

5.5 SECTION VIEWS

The cutaway view of a device appeared first in various forms in the 15th and 16th centuries to show details of parts hidden by other elements. These cutaway views have evolved to ***section views*** in which interior features that cannot be effectively displayed by hidden lines are exposed by slicing through a section of the object. To create a section view, a cutting plane is passed through the part and the portion of the part on one side of the cutting plane is imagined to be removed. In a section view, all visible edges and contours behind the cutting plane are shown. Hidden lines are usually omitted. The portion of the object that is sliced through is designated with angled crosshatch lines known as section lining.

Section views are easily demonstrated by considering a block with a hole that has a large diameter part way into it and a smaller diameter through the remainder of it, as shown in Figure 5.10a. In this case, the object is sectioned along a cutting plane parallel to the right and left sides of the block and through the center of the hole, as indicated in Figure 5.10b. If the right half is cut away, the remaining portion of the object looks like Figure 5.10c, revealing the cross section at the cut that clearly shows the two diameters of the hole. In a drawing, the cross section is defined and shown schematically by using two views, as shown in Figure 5.10d. Key to the interpretation of a section view is the clear representation of where the cutting plane is and from which direction it is viewed. This is accomplished using a ***cutting plane line*** (long dash, short dash, short dash, long dash, with perpendicular arrows at each end). The cutting plane line, A-A, shows where the cutting plane passes through the object in the front orthographic view. The arrows on either end of the cutting plane line show the direction of the ***line of sight*** for the section view. Thus, the section view shown to the right of the front view is what the viewer would see if the portion of the object that is "behind" the direction that the arrows are pointing is removed. The section view is placed to the right of the front view to be consistent with the convention of the third-angle projection (as if unfolding the glass box after the portion of the object is removed). The two diameters of the hole are evident, with the surface where the material has been "cut" away shown as ***crosshatched*** having angled, parallel lines drawn on the surface that was cut. This view is designated SECTION A-A to correspond to the cutting plane line A-A. This type of section in which a single plane goes completely through an object is known as a ***full section***.

cutting plane

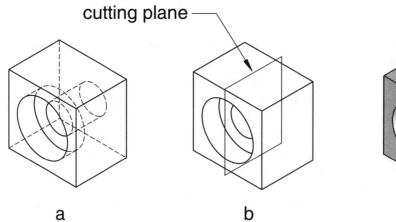 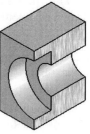

a   b   c

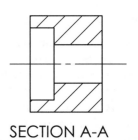

A

A

SECTION A-A

Figure 5.10
Creating a section view.

d

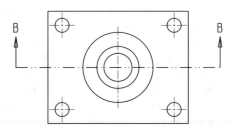

B   B

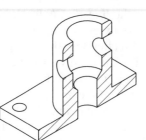 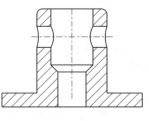

Figure 5.11
The full section is the
orthographic view at the
lower right.

SECTION B-B

A slightly more complicated example of a full section is shown in Figure 5.11. The whole object is shown in the upper-left portion of the figure, and the sectioned object is shown with a portion removed just below it. The right side of the figure shows a top view of the object with the cutting plane displayed. Imagine that the material on the side of the cutting plane in the direction the arrows are pointing is retained, and the material behind the arrows is removed. Then the projection of the retained portion appears as SECTION B-B when viewed in the direction of the arrows.

Much more sophisticated section views can be created for complicated parts. In all cases, though, clear definition of the cutting plane line and the direction of the line of sight for the view are critical. For example, Figure 5.12 shows a *half section* of the same part. The cutting plane extends halfway through the object to show the interior of one half of the object and the exterior of the other half. This type of section is ideal for symmetrical parts in which it is desired to show internal and external features in a single view. When only a portion of the object needs to be sectioned to show a particular internal detail, a *broken-out section* like that shown in Figure 5.13 can be used. A break line separates the sectioned portion from the unsectioned portion, but no cutting plane line is drawn.

An *offset section* like that shown in Figure 5.14 is used to show internal details that are not in the same plane. The cutting plane for offset sections is bent at 90° angles to pass through important features. Only the segments of the cross section that would be visible when projected along the line of sight are shown in section H-H; the changes of plane that occur at the 90° offsets are not represented with lines on the section view. A variation of the offset section is the *aligned section*. The holes in the triangular object shown in Figure 5.15a are different from one another. However, the orthographic projections in Figure 5.15b cannot show the holes clearly, because the hidden lines overlap in the standard views. The aligned section shown in Figure 5.15c clearly distinguishes the three different hole styles. Unlike the offset section, which shows only the segments of the cross section that are projected and

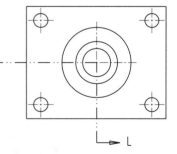

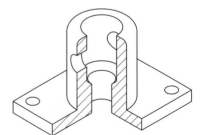

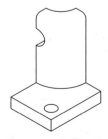

Removed Portion

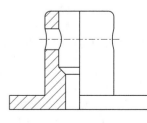

SECTION   L-L

Figure 5.12
The half section is the orthographic view at the lower right.

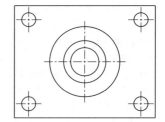

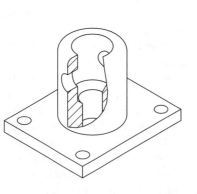

Figure 5.13
The broken-out section is the orthographic view at the lower right.

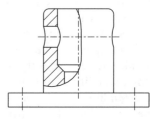

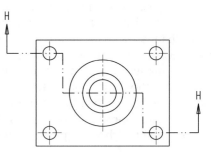

Figure 5.14
The offset section is the orthographic view at the lower right. Note that the horizontal holes in the cylindrical upper portion of the part have curved edges in the section view due to the shape of the part, whereas the vertical holes in the flat flange at the bottom of the part have straight edges.

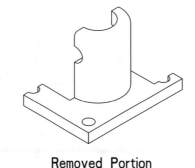

Removed Portion

SECTION H-H

visible along the line of sight, the aligned section stretches out the offset segments of the cross section side by side into a single plane and projects them as if they were a full section. This makes the overall length of the aligned section in Figure 5.15c longer than the length of the bottom side of the front view in Figure 5.15b. As a result, an aligned view cannot be projected directly from the front view. Again, the 90° offsets are not shown on the section view.

Sometimes it is helpful to show the cross section at a certain point along the length of an object. One way to do this is with a ***removed section***, shown in Figure 5.16. In this case the cross section of the contoured handle at the point indicated by the section line is displayed. Often, removed sections are used to show a slice at a

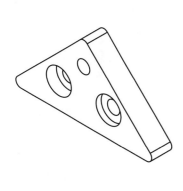

a

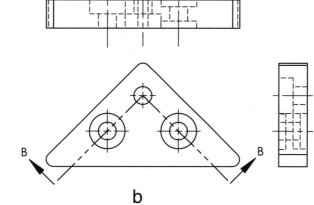

b

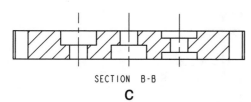

SECTION B-B

c

Figure 5.15
The aligned section is shown in (c).

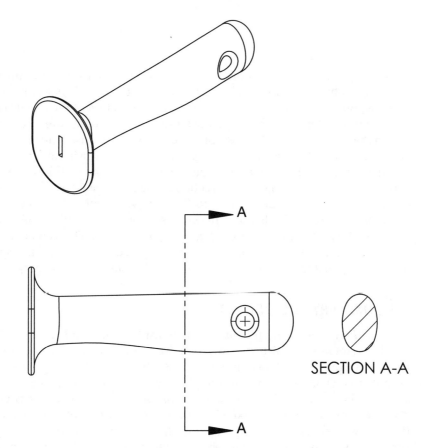

SECTION A-A

Figure 5.16
The removed section is shown to the side of the part.

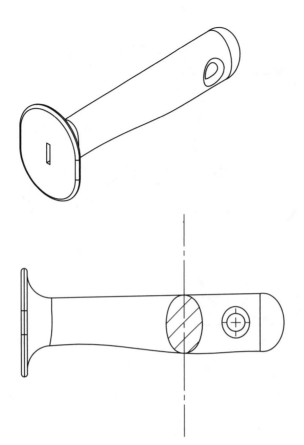

Figure 5.17
The revolved section is superimposed on the part.

point along the length of an object that indicates the contour of a complicated shape. Although only one removed section is shown in Figure 5.16, several other removed sections could be displayed to show how the cross section of the handle changes from point to point along its length. Removed sections are a bit different from a full section in that they need not be positioned according to the usual alignment of views. In addition, removed sections are often *partial views* in which only the section itself is shown without displaying features that are not part of the section, but would normally be visible when viewing in the direction of the line of sight as defined by the arrows of the section line. An alternative to the removed section is the ***revolved section***, shown in Figure 5.17. In this case, the cross section is revolved 90° and then superimposed on the part at the position where the part is sliced. This can be quite helpful to show the shape of the cross section of an elongated feature such as a spoke, web, or aircraft wing that might not be apparent from the standard orthographic views.

5.6 AUXILIARY AND DETAIL VIEWS

An ***auxiliary view*** is often convenient to display the details of a part that are not readily visible or are distorted when viewed in one of the principal orthographic views. An example is shown in Figure 5.18. The sloped surface A has a large circular hole that is perpendicular to the plane, which is shown as a pair of parallel hidden lines in the front view. However, from the top view or the right view, the hole does not appear circular. Likewise, surface A is not displayed at its true size in these views, because it is not parallel to the plane of the paper. The only time that surface A will have true size and shape is when it is viewed along a line of sight that

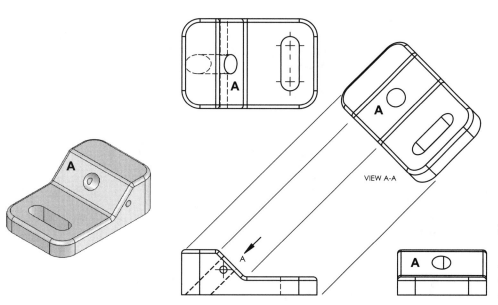

Figure 5.18
Auxiliary view of plane A.
The labels A on the isometric projection and on the auxiliary and right views are not included on standard drawings.

is perpendicular to the plane. To show the true size and shape of surface A and the large hole, an auxiliary view is created. The line of sight, indicated by the arrow with A next to it in the front view, is perpendicular to the inclined surface A. The fine construction lines parallel to the line of sight define the alignment of the edges between the front view and the auxiliary view A. In this auxiliary view, surface A is parallel to the paper. Notice that the surface and the hole are not distorted: surface A is its true size and shape, and the hole in the surface appears circular. Creating an auxiliary view manually is challenging, but CAD software makes the process quite simple. Often all that is necessary is to identify an edge, in this case the edge of surface A in the front view, and indicate that an auxiliary view is desired. The software automatically creates the view and positions it properly.

Note that some details, such as center marks for the holes and rounded edges, as well as some hidden lines, have been omitted in Figure 5.18. This was done to aid in clarity of the drawing. This is a common practice in engineering drawings. The key is to provide the maximum clarity in the drawing while retaining all of the information that is necessary to create the object. Sometimes this requires omitting confusing lines, marks, or symbols.

In some cases, it is necessary to make clear details of the part that are not readily evident in the views normally shown in the drawing. For instance, a particular detail may be so small that it cannot be shown clearly on the same scale as the remainder of the part. This is done using an auxiliary ***detail view*** consisting of a small portion of the object magnified to make the small feature clear. An example is shown in Figure 5.19. In this case the small rivet holding the blade onto the arms of the pizza cutter is too small to see in the orthographic views. The region of interest near the rivet is circled in the leftmost projection of the pizza cutter, which is a full-section view. The letter B on the circle directs the reader to a magnified detail view B in the upper-right part of the drawing. The cross section of the rivet is clearly visible in this detail view. Since several parts are shown in cross section, a variety of ***crosshatch lines***, also known as ***section lines***, with different angles and spacing between the lines are used to distinguish one part from another. Generally, the crosshatch lines are drawn at a 45° angle and spaced about $\frac{1}{16}$ inch, or 1.5 mm, apart. However, to avoid confusion with visible lines, it is important that the crosshatch lines be drawn so that they are not parallel to any visible

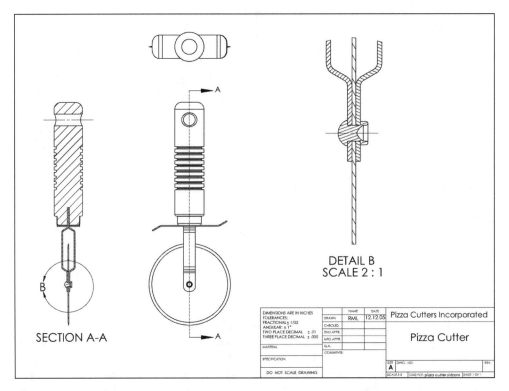

Figure 5.19
Detail view of a small section of an assembly.

lines of the bounding area that is crosshatched. In the detail view in Figure 5.19, the orientations of the crosshatch lines have been carefully adjusted so that none are parallel to visible lines. Furthermore, crosshatch lines perpendicular to visible lines of the bounding area should be avoided. It is also important that the crosshatch lines for separate portions of a single part be the same. For example, the section lines for individual parts are the same above and below the rivet in Figure 5.19. Usually standard parts such as fasteners, washers, springs, bearings, and gears are not crosshatched. But in the case of Figure 5.19, the rivet detail is integral to the assembly, so it is helpful to show its cross section with crosshatching to indicate how it fits with the other parts. Crosshatching can be used to designate the type of material, although this is not frequently done. ANSI standard section lines for a variety of materials are shown in Figure 5.20. In most CAD software, the selection of the type of crosshatching is quite easy.

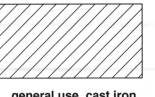 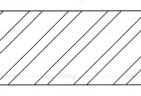 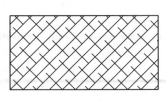

general use, cast iron   **steel**   **aluminum**

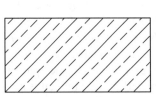 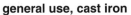 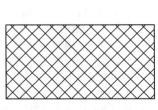

Figure 5.20
ANSI standard section lines for several materials.

brass, bronze   **zinc, lead, magnesium**   **plastic, rubber**

5.7 FASTENERS AND SCREW THREADS

Fasteners include a broad range of items such as bolts, nuts, screws, and rivets used to "fasten" parts together. In most cases, fasteners are standard parts purchased from an outside vendor, so detail drawings of fasteners are rarely necessary. Nevertheless, threaded holes and threaded shafts are sometimes represented on a drawing.

The geometry of screw threads is too complicated to draw exactly in an engineering drawing and screw threads are standard, so either of two simple conventions is used to indicate screw threads, as shown in Figure 5.21. The *schematic representation* is used when a realistic representation of the side view of a screw thread is desired. For an external thread, the lines that extend across the entire diameter represent the *crest*, or peak, of the thread, while the shorter lines in between represent the *root*, or valley, of the thread. The distance between crests or between roots is called the *pitch*. On a drawing, the crests and roots are shown perpendicular to the axis of the threaded section rather than helical as they actually appear on the physical thread. In the end view, threads are depicted with concentric circles. The outer circle is the largest diameter of the screw thread, known as the *major diameter*, and the inner circle is the smallest diameter of the screw thread, or *minor diameter*. In the end view of the external thread, both diameters are shown as solid circles. In the *simplified representation* of external screw threads, the threads are omitted altogether. The major diameter is represented as a solid line in the side view, and the minor diameter is represented with a dashed line.

The end view of an internal thread is shown as two concentric circles representing the major and minor diameter, but the major diameter is a hidden line. For a side view of a hidden internal screw thread, the major and minor diameters are both shown as hidden lines for both schematic and simplified screw thread representations.

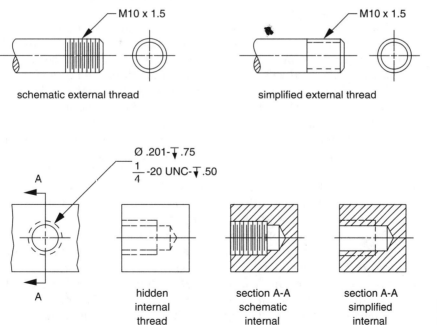

schematic external thread   simplified external thread

hidden internal thread   section A-A schematic internal thread   section A-A simplified internal thread

Figure 5.21
Conventions to show screw threads.

In a cross section, internal threads can be shown in either the schematic or the simplified representation, as shown. For a hole that does not go completely through the part, called a *blind hole*, the lines in the side view representing the minor diameter continue deeper than the thread and come to a point. This represents the hole that is drilled prior to tapping, or cutting threads in the hole. The hole needs to be longer than the threaded section to permit the tool that is used to cut the threads, or tap, to penetrate deeply enough to fully cut the threads in the portion of the hole to be tapped.

Screw threads are specified in terms of the nominal (major) diameter, the pitch, and the thread series. For instance, the designations $\frac{1}{4}$-20 UNC, .25-20 UNC, or $\frac{1}{4}$-20 NC all indicate a major diameter of .25 inch, a pitch of 20 threads per inch, and the Unified Coarse (UNC) series. The diameter of the hole drilled before tapping an internal thread is specified in a wide variety of machinist and engineering handbooks. In this case, the proper hole to be drilled has a diameter of .2010 inch, which corresponds to a number 7 drill. To make an internal thread of this size, a machinist would first drill a hole using a number 7 drill bit and then cut the threads using a $\frac{1}{4}$-20 tap. For screw threads with a nominal diameter less than .25 inch, a number designation is used to specify the nominal diameter. For example, the designation 10-32 UNF indicates a nominal diameter of .1900 inch, 32 threads per inch, and the Unified Fine (UNF) series. The pitch is equal to 1 divided by the number of threads per inch.

Metric threads are specified in a slightly different way. A designation M10 × 1.5 indicates a metric thread with a 10-mm major diameter and a pitch of 1.5 mm between crests of the thread. The number of threads per mm is 1 divided by the pitch. Other letters and numbers may follow the thread specification to denote tolerances and deviations of the thread, but for many cases these are not necessary. In addition, for a blind hole, the depth of the thread can be specified in several ways. Following the thread designation, the notation X .50 DEEP, THD .50 DP, or a downward arrow with a horizontal bar at its tail followed by .50 all indicate that the thread should extend .50 inch below the surface of the piece, as shown in Figure 5.21. (THD indicates "thread," and DP indicates "deep.") The threaded depth is usually 1.5 to 2 times the nominal diameter of the screw thread.

The dimensions for a threaded hole are indicated on a drawing using a leader line with the arrow pointing at the major diameter, as shown in Figure 5.21. Threaded holes are usually dimensioned in the view where they appear as circles, rather than in a side view of the threaded hole. Multiple threaded holes of the same specification are typically denoted in the same way as other multiple features using the notation (2X) or 2 TIMES at the end of the thread designation.

Bolts, which are often called machine screws, and nuts are usually shown only in a parts list and are not included on any drawings, except perhaps an assembly drawing. Nuts and bolts are specified in the same way as threaded holes, plus a bolt length and the type of head. For instance .25-28 UNF X 1.50 HEXAGON CAP SCREW or .25-28 NF X 1.50 HEX CAP SCR indicates a .25-28 Unified Fine series bolt that is 1.5 inches long with hexagonal head. Nuts are specified in terms of their thread and shape, such as M8 X 1.25 HEX NUT.

Frequently the top of a threaded hole is designed so that the head of the bolt is flush with or slightly below the surface. This is called a *counterbore hole* or a *countersink hole*, depending on the shape of the head of the bolt. A counterbore hole has an enlarged cylindrical portion at the top of the hole, to accept the head of a bolt, as shown in the leftmost hole in Section A-A of Figure 5.22. A countersink hole has a conical taper at the top of the hole, shown as the middle hole in Figure 5.22, to accept the conical head of a countersink, flat-head screw. These two holes

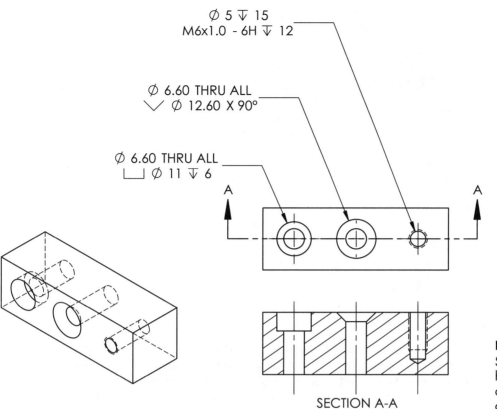

Ø 5 ⍗ 15
M6x1.0 - 6H ⍗ 12

Ø 6.60 THRU ALL
⌵ Ø 12.60 X 90°

Ø 6.60 THRU ALL
⌴ Ø 11 ⍗ 6

A   A

SECTION A-A

Figure 5.22
Showing counterbore
holes, countersink holes,
and threaded holes on a
drawing.

are dimensioned for a metric M6 bolt. In both cases, the through hole has a diameter of 6.60 mm, designated on the drawing as Ø 6.60 THRU ALL. This diameter is large enough that the bolt slides easily into the hole, but is not loose in the hole. The second line of the dimension of the hole indicates the size of the counterbore or countersink. For the counterbore, the U-shaped symbol indicates a U-shaped counterbore at the top of the hole. The diameter of the counterbore is 11 mm and the depth, indicated by the downward arrow, is 6 mm. The countersink is designated with a V-shaped symbol. The diameter of 12.60 mm is the diameter at the top of the conical taper, and the 90 angle is the angle formed at the point of the conical taper.

While this all seems quite complicated, CAD software makes it quite easy to specify a counterbore or countersink by using a menu such as the example shown in Figure 5.23. All that is needed is to specify the shape of the hole (the upper-left button showing a counterbore), the engineering standard for the bolt (ANSI Metric), the type of bolt (Socket Head Cap Screw), the bolt size (M6), the tightness of the through hole (Close, Normal, Loose), and the depth of the hole (Through All). Given this information, the CAD software automatically determines the appropriate diameter, depth, and other specifications for the hole based on standard engineering practice. When the hole is dimensioned in a drawing, this information automatically appears, as shown in Figure 5.22. Threaded holes can be specified in a similar way. All that is needed is the engineering standard for the thread (ANSI Metric), the thread designation (M6 × 1.0), and the depth into the hole that the thread should extend (12 mm). From this, the CAD software automatically determines the size of the hole to be drilled prior to tapping

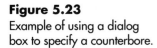

Figure 5.23
Example of using a dialog
box to specify a counterbore.

and the depth that the hole needs to be drilled so that the hole can be tapped to the specified depth. The depth of the hole is the depth of the cylindrical section of the hole, not the depth to the point of the conical portion of the hole. Once specified, this information appears automatically on the drawing, with the first line of the dimension indicating the drill diameter (5 mm) and depth (15 mm) and the second line indicating the thread specification (M6 × 1.0) and the depth for the threads (12 mm), as shown for the rightmost hole in Figure 5.22. The 6H in the second line indicates a standard thread tolerance grade specifying how much the dimensions of the thread can deviate from the standard dimensions for this thread size.

5.8 ASSEMBLY DRAWINGS

An assembly drawing shows all of the components of a design either assembled or in an exploded view. Many times assembly drawings include sections. Most dimensions are omitted in assembly drawings. Individual parts are not dimensioned, but some dimensions of the assembled mechanism may be included. Hidden lines are seldom necessary in assembly drawings, although they can be used where they clarify the design. Leader lines attached to a ballooned letter or detail number, as shown in Figure 5.24, reference the parts of the assembly. The leader lines should not cross and nearby leader lines should be approximately parallel. Sometimes parts are labeled by name rather than number. The parts list may be on the assembly drawing (usually on the right side or at the bottom) or it may be a separate sheet. The assembly drawing may also include machining or assembly information in the form of notes on the drawing. Often assembly drawings include assembly sections. These are typically orthographic or pictorial section views of parts as put together in an assembly. The assembly cross section on the left side of Figure 5.19 shows the interior structure of the parts of a pizza cutter and how they fit together. The detail view in the upper right of Figure 5.19 shows the cross section through the rivet to indicate how the parts are assembled.

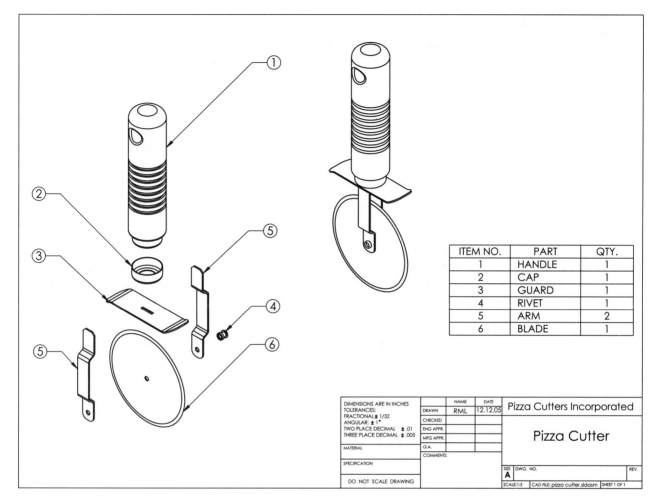

ITEM NO.	PART	QTY.
1	HANDLE	1
2	CAP	1
3	GUARD	1
4	RIVET	1
5	ARM	2
6	BLADE	1

DIMENSIONS ARE IN INCHES
TOLERANCES:
FRACTIONAL± 1/32
ANGULAR: ± 1°
TWO PLACE DECIMAL   ± .01
THREE PLACE DECIMAL   ± .005

MATERIAL

SPECIFICATION

DO NOT SCALE DRAWING

	NAME	DATE
DRAWN	RML	12.12.05
CHECKED		
ENG APPR.		
MFG APPR.		
Q.A.		
COMMENTS:		

Pizza Cutters Incorporated

Pizza Cutter

SIZE **A**   DWG. NO.   REV.

SCALE:1:3   CAD FILE: pizza cutter.sldasm   SHEET 1 OF 1

Figure 5.24
Assembly drawing of a pizza cutter.

KEY TERMS

Aligned section
ANSI
Auxiliary view
Blind hole
Broken-out section
Center mark
Centerlines
Contour dimensioning
Counterbore hole
Countersink hole
Crest
Crosshatch lines
Cutting plane lines
Detail view

Dimension lines
Extension lines
Full section
Half section
Hidden lines
ISO
Leader lines
Line of sight
Major diameter
Minor diameter
Offset section
Overdimensioned
Partial view
Pitch

Precedence of lines
Reference dimension
Removed section
Revolved section
Root
Scale
Section lines
Section views
Sheet layout
Title block
Visible lines
Witness lines

PROBLEMS

5.1 Three orthographic views and an isometric projection of an object that has overall dimensions of 4 × 4 × 4 inches are to be shown in a drawing. Determine the best ANSI sheet size for an object of this size at the scales indicated below:

(a) Half size.

(b) 2:1.

(c) 1 = 1.

5.2 Three orthographic views and an isometric projection of an object that has overall dimensions of 200 × 200 × 200 mm are to be shown in a drawing. Determine the optimal standard metric scale to be used for the ISO sheet sizes indicated below:

(a) A1.

(b) A3.

(c) A4.

5.3 The drawing shown in Figure 5.25 has many errors in the dimensioning. Sketch or draw with CAD the orthographic views and show the proper placement of the dimensions.

5.4 The drawing shown in Figure 5.26 has many errors in the dimensioning. Sketch or draw with CAD the orthographic views and show the proper placement of the dimensions. The M10 × 1.5 threaded hole requires a tap drill of 8.5 mm. Only two views are needed for this part.

5.5 The drawing shown in Figure 5.27 is dimensioned using the ISO standard, which has a slightly different look than most dimensions used in this chapter, which use the ANSI standard. However, there are many errors in the dimensioning. Sketch

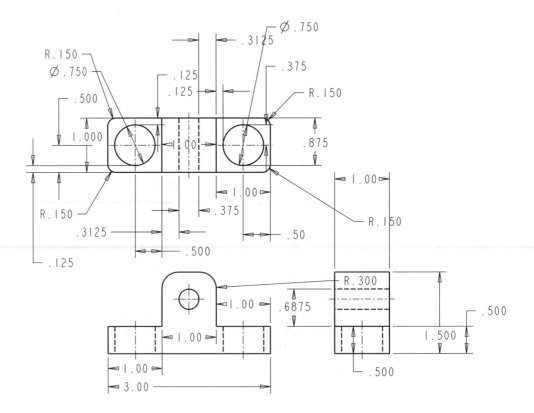

Figure 5.25

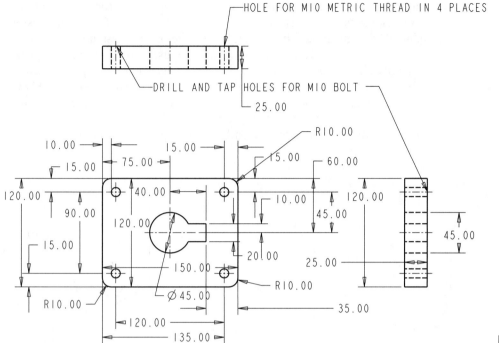

Figure 5.26

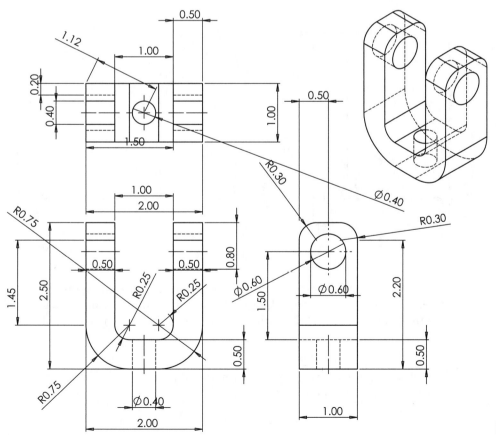

Figure 5.27

or draw with CAD the orthographic views and show the proper placement of the dimensions, using the ISO standard in which the values for the dimensions are aligned with the dimension line and set above the dimension line.

5.6 The drawing shown in Figure 5.28 is dimensioned using the ISO standard, which has a slightly different look than most dimensions used in this chapter, which use the ANSI standard. However, there are many errors in the dimensioning. Sketch or draw with CAD the orthographic views and show the proper placement of the dimensions, using the ISO standard in which the values for the dimensions are aligned with the dimension line and set above the dimension line.

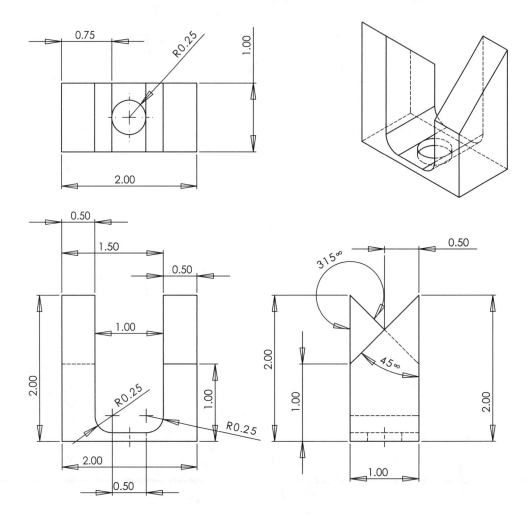

Figure 5.28

5.7 Sketch the following section views for the object shown in Figure 5.29. The threaded holes extend from the top surface approximately halfway through the thickness of the part. The other holes extend through the part.

(a) A-A.

(b) B-B.

5.8 Sketch the following section views for the object shown in Figure 5.30. All holes extend through the part.

(a) B-B.

(b) D-D.

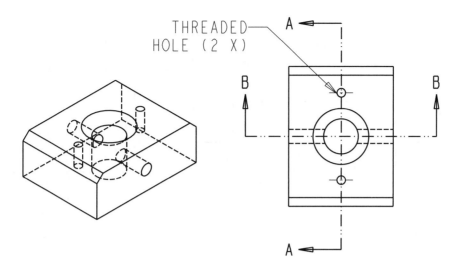

THREADED HOLE (2 X)

A

B   B

A

Isometric View   Top View   **Figure 5.29**

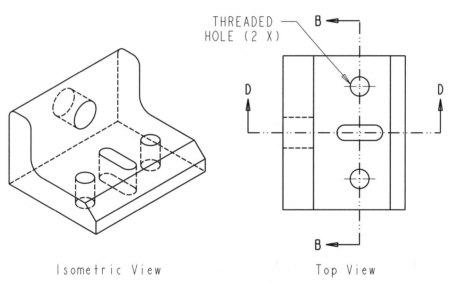

THREADED HOLE (2 X)

B

D   D

B

Isometric View   Top View   **Figure 5.30**

5.9   Sketch or draw with CAD section A-A for the object shown in Figure 5.31 using the dimensions in Figure 5.28.

5.10   Sketch the following section views for the object shown in Figure 5.32. All holes extend through the part.

    (a) A-A.

    (b) C-C.

5.11   Figure 5.33, a–f, shows the dimensioned front view and several different corresponding right-side views, each with a horizontal width of 1 inch. Using CAD, draw three orthographic views (front, top, and right side) as well as the auxiliary view of the inclined surface for the corresponding right-side view.

5.12   Look up the following machine screw threads in an engineering graphics book (such as *Engineering Graphics* by Giesecke, et al.), a machinist's or engineering handbook (such as *Marks' Standard Handbook for Mechanical Engineers*),

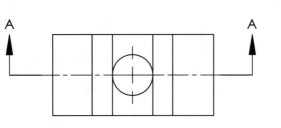

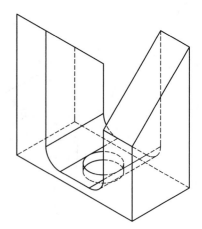

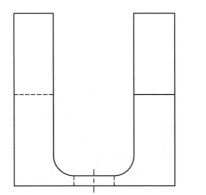

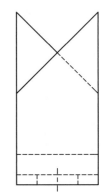

Figure 5.31

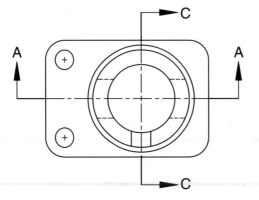

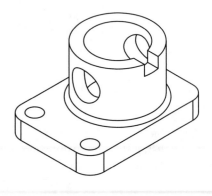

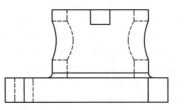

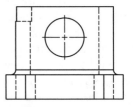

Figure 5.32

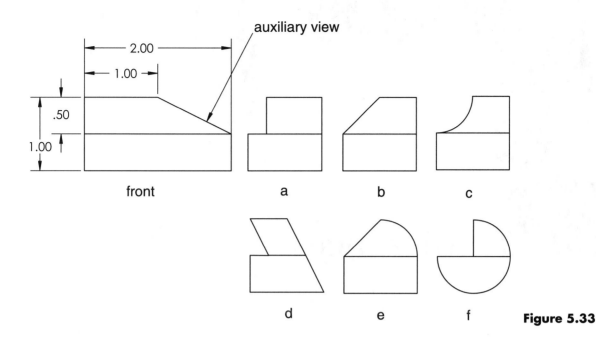

Figure 5.33

an industrial supply catalog (such as McMaster-Carr), or on the Internet (search on "tap drill size"). Specify the series (UNC or UNF), tap drill size or number, number of threads per inch, pitch, and nominal diameter.

(a) 4-40.

(b) 6-32.

(c) 8-32.

(d) $\frac{3}{8}$-24.

(e) 6-40.

(f) $\frac{1}{4}$-28.

5.13 Look up the following machine screw threads in an engineering graphics book (such as *Engineering Graphics* by Giesecke, et al.), a machinist's or engineering handbook (such as *Marks' Standard Handbook for Mechanical Engineers*), an industrial supply catalog (such as McMaster-Carr), or on the Internet (search on "tap drill size metric"). Specify the series (course or fine), tap drill size, number of threads per mm, and nominal size.

(a) M2 × 0.4.

(b) M12 × 1.75.

(c) M30 × 3.5.

(d) M30 × 2.

(e) M10 × 1.25.

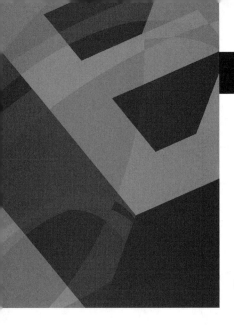

Tolerances

Objectives

After reading this chapter, you should be able to

- Explain interchangeable parts
- Explain why tolerancing is necessary
- Read a general tolerance on a drawing
- Read limit dimensions and tolerances on individual dimensions
- Determine a tolerance stackup
- Determine the range of tolerances for manufacturing processes
- Explain the differences between clearance, interference, and transition fits
- Read a surface finish specification
- Understand basic form tolerances
- Understand simple positional tolerances
- Read geometric dimensioning and tolerancing symbols

OVERVIEW

Tolerances on dimensions are necessary to specify the acceptable variability in the dimension of a part. Tolerances can be indicated for all dimensions using a general note or they can be specified for each individual dimension. Tolerances are based on the function of the part or are used to ensure that mating parts fit together. However, in many cases the manufacturing process determines the tolerance. The surface finish may also be specified on a drawing to indicate the roughness of the surface. To further minimize ambiguity in engineering drawings, geometric dimensioning and tolerancing is used to specify the form of a feature, such as flatness or roundness, or to indicate the ideal position of a feature.

6.1 WHY TOLERANCES?

In 1815, it was hoped that muskets could be produced in a number of different U. S. Government and private armories so that the parts of the musket would be interchangeable. Before that time, muskets were individually handcrafted, so parts from one musket rarely fit another musket. Because engineering drawings were not commonly used, a number of "perfect" muskets were made according to master gauges and jigs. *Gauges* are devices used to check the individual dimensions of a part. For instance, the diameter of a shaft can be checked using a gauge consisting of two holes: one of the maximum allowable diameter of the shaft and one of the minimum allowable diameter. If the shaft fits through the larger hole, but not the smaller hole, then it is within the allowable dimensions for the shaft. *Jigs* are devices used to hold a workpiece and guide the tool to ensure repeatable machining. The master gauges and jigs were sent to the armories with the instruction that "no deviations from the pattern were to be allowed." In 1824, this concept of *interchangeable parts* was tested by disassembling a hundred rifles from several different armories, mixing the parts, and then reassembling the parts at random. Most reassembled rifles worked as they should, proving the concept and value of interchangeable parts.

The interchangeability of parts is so common now that it is hard to imagine anything different. The concept allows parts made in various locations by different manufacturers to be successfully assembled and to function properly as an assembly. Although engineering drawings rather than "master parts" came into use in the mid-19th century, it was the two world wars in the 20th century that brought about the development of methods of showing the acceptable variation in a dimension on a drawing, or *tolerancing*.

The need to control precisely the geometry of a part arises from the part's function. For instance, the cross-sectional geometry of an airfoil, such as the wing of a jet aircraft or a turbine blade, must be accurately controlled to ensure aerodynamic efficiency. The more commonplace need for controlling geometry results from the requirement for parts to fit together. But it is quite difficult to make every part the exact size that is specified in a dimension because of slight differences in tool size, machine tool wear, human operator error, and other factors. As a consequence, tolerances are used in engineering drawings to specify the limit in the variation between mating parts and to provide guidelines to control the manufacturing process. The *tolerance* is the amount that a specific dimension is permitted to vary, or the difference between the maximum and minimum limits of a dimension.

Consider a dimension on a drawing specified as $3.750 \pm .003$. This dimension indicates that the part has a *nominal size*, or general size, of $3\frac{3}{4}$ inches (usually expressed as a common fraction). The *basic size*, or theoretical size for the application of the tolerance, is 3.750 inches (expressed as a decimal). The tolerance of the dimension is .006 inch. Thus, an acceptable machined part can have an *actual size* ranging from 3.747 to 3.753 inches, which are the minimum and maximum limits of the dimension. If the actual size is smaller than 3.747 or larger than 3.753, then the part is not acceptable.

Of course, it is desirable to make the part as close as possible to the basic size, sometimes called the *target size*. But the more accuracy needed in a machined part, the higher is the manufacturing cost. Furthermore, the method of machining a part limits the tolerance that can be specified. For instance, the tolerance in drilling a .500-inch hole is between .002 and .005 depending on the quality of the drill press and drill bit. To require a tolerance smaller than .002 would require an additional machining process, such as reaming. Consequently, tolerances can play a large role in the cost of manufacturing a part. Therefore, the tolerances should not be specified tighter than necessary for the product to function properly.

An increased awareness of the importance of tolerances in manufacturing has led to an approach in which the deviation of the actual size of a part from the target size has a cost in terms of reworking of the part, scrap, customer dissatisfaction, and poor reliability. An approach to handle this is to design a product so that it is less sensitive to manufacturing tolerances. The idea is to design the part intelligently so that easy-to-manufacture tolerances, rather than exceptionally tight tolerances, are implemented. Consequently, proper fit between mating parts comes about because of good design, instead of depending on tight tolerances. This approach is known as *robust design*.

6.2 DISPLAYING TOLERANCES ON DRAWINGS

Every dimension on a drawing should have a tolerance. Tolerances can be displayed on engineering drawings in several ways depending on the situation.

General tolerances can be given in a note on the drawing or in the title block. An example would be the note ALL DIMENSIONS TO BE HELD TO $\pm.003''$.

Thus, a dimension of .375 would have a minimum limit of .372 and a maximum limit of .378. Often general tolerances are specified in terms of the number of digits following the decimal point in a dimension. In this case, a note would appear on the drawing, such as

UNLESS OTHERWISE SPECIFIED

TOL: .XX = ±.010

.XXX = ±.005

HOLES = ±.002

ANGLES = ±.5 DEG

Thus, a dimension of .50 on a drawing would indicate an actual size between .490 and .510. A dimension of .500 would indicate an actual size between .495 and .505. For metric dimension, a similar form for general tolerances would be X.X METRIC = ±.08.

Two other methods of displaying tolerances on a drawing are shown in Figure 6.1. The maximum and minimum sizes are specified directly when using *limit dimensions* to specify the tolerance. Usually the upper limit is placed above the lower limit. While this method clearly shows the limits of the dimension, many engineers, designers, and machinists think in terms of the nominal or basic size plus a tolerance, neither of which is immediately evident using limit dimensions. Thus, a more common approach is to use *plus and minus dimensions* where the basic size is shown followed by the tolerance values. If the plus and minus tolerance values are identical, then the basic dimension is followed by a plus-or-minus sign and half of the numerical value of the tolerance. Otherwise, the plus and minus tolerances are indicated separately with the plus above the minus. A *bilateral tolerance*, such as the tolerance for the 1.500-inch dimension in Figure 6.1, varies equally in both directions from the basic size. A *unilateral tolerance*, such as the tolerance for the 1.250 diameter of the shaft in Figure 6.1, varies in only one direction from the basic size. In both cases, the number of digits to the right of the decimal point for the dimension should be the same as the number of digits to the right of the decimal point for the tolerance.

Sometimes it is not necessary to specify both limits of a tolerance, and only one limit dimension is needed. MIN or MAX is placed after a numerical dimension to indicate that it is a *single-limit dimension*. The depth of holes, length of threads, and radii of corner rounds are often specified using single-limit dimensions.

Many times several methods of representing tolerances are used on a single drawing. For instance, general tolerances may be listed in the title block, and plus and minus dimensions or limit dimensions may be used for a few dimensions to which the general tolerances do not apply.

An important consideration in applying tolerances is the effect of one tolerance on another, especially because tolerances are cumulative. This is known as

Figure 6.1
Plus and minus tolerances and limit tolerances.

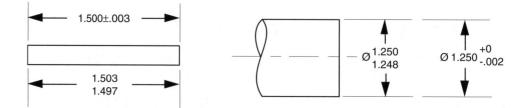

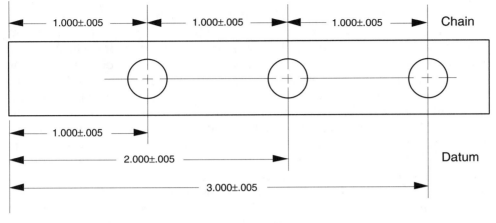

Figure 6.2
Chain dimensioning and datum dimensioning.

tolerance accumulation or *tolerance stackup* for a chain of dimensions. In the example in Figure 6.2, two dimensioning schemes are shown. Above the part, *chain dimensioning* shows the distance from one feature to the next. This would be an appropriate dimensioning scheme if the distance from one hole to the next was critical, because the distance between holes must be between .995 and 1.005. But if the distances of the holes from the left edge of the part were critical, a large tolerance would accumulate. The third hole would be 2.985 from the left edge if all of the dimensions happened to be at the minimum limit of the dimension, or 3.015 from the left edge if all dimensions were at the maximum limit. Thus, the actual dimension of the third hole from the left edge using chain dimensioning is 3.000 ± .015. This tolerance accumulation can be avoided using *datum dimensioning*, where the dimensions are given with respect to a datum, in this case the left edge of the part as shown below the part in Figure 6.2. Using this scheme, the third hole is specified to be between 2.995 and 3.005 from the left edge. Of course, the distance between the second and third holes could be as small as .990 if the second hole is at 2.005 and the third hole is at 2.995. Alternatively, the distance between the second and third holes could be as large as 1.010 if the holes are at 1.995 and 3.005. Consequently, the decision about which way to dimension the holes depends on whether the distance between holes is critical or whether the distance from each hole to the left edge is critical.

6.3 HOW TO DETERMINE TOLERANCES

One of the most difficult aspects of dimensioning and tolerancing for inexperienced engineers and designers is to determine what tolerance to specify on a drawing. In some cases a specific tolerance is quite clear based on the function of the design. For instance, if a $\frac{3}{4}$-inch shaft must rotate at moderate speed in a hole, the tolerances on the shaft and the hole can be determined based on standard classes of fits that are available in many engineering and machinist handbooks. In this particular case the hole could be between .7500 and .7512, while the shaft could have a diameter of .7484 to .7492. A shaft any bigger or a hole any smaller would result in too tight of a clearance for the shaft to rotate freely, or could result in the shaft being too big for the hole. A smaller shaft or larger hole than the specified limits would result in a sloppy fit between the shaft and the hole. The point here is not the details of how the tolerances are determined. That is too specific to individual cases for this discussion and is presented in many handbooks and texts. Instead, the point is that the function of the system that is being designed drives the tolerances. In this case, *the tolerances drive the manufacturing process* used to machine the hole and the shaft.

But a more common situation is the opposite: *The manufacturing process drives the tolerance.* If the only machine tool that is available to form a hole is a drill press, the $\frac{3}{4}$-inch hole that is cut will be between .748 and .754 in diameter based on expected tolerances for the drilling operation. But this means that the hole in the example just presented would have too much variability to ensure that the shaft rotates in it properly. Of course, if only one shaft-hole assembly was being made, the hole could be drilled first and measured. Then the shaft could be turned on a lathe to a diameter just slightly smaller to achieve the fit described. However, this approach will clearly not work for mass-produced, interchangeable parts. Either a more accurate machining method is needed to create the hole or the design must be altered to avoid drilling a hole altogether. (In this example, a standard-size, off-the-shelf bearing could be inserted into a larger drilled hole to mate with the shaft.)

When the manufacturing processes that are available drive the tolerances, the tolerances on the drawing must reflect the manufacturing process that is used to make the part, and the design must be altered to ensure that the part can be made with the available machining processes. Guidelines are available for the tolerance range of various common machining processes, including the following:

Lapping: A process that produces a very smooth and accurate surface by rubbing the surface of the workpiece against a mating form, often using a fine abrasive between the surfaces.

Honing: A process in which a honing stone made of fine abrasive is used to form a surface on a workpiece.

Grinding: A process that removes a small amount of material from a workpiece with a rapidly rotating grinding wheel.

Broaching: A process similar to filing in which a cutting tool is reciprocated along its axis to remove a small amount of material from a workpiece.

Reaming: Removal of a small amount of material from a drilled hole using a rotating cutting tool (reamer).

Turning: Axisymmetric removal of material from a rotating workpiece by feeding a cutting tool into the workpiece using a lathe.

Boring: Axisymmetric removal of material from a workpiece using a tool with a single cutting surface. Either the workpiece or the tool may be rotating.

Milling: Removal of material by feeding a workpiece into a rotating cutting tool.

Drilling: Creating a hole by feeding the end of a sharpened cylindrical cutting tool (drill bit) into the material.

Stamping and *Punching:* Cutting material using a punch and a die to shear the material, much like a paper hole-punch.

The tolerance typically depends on the size of the feature, as well as the quality of the machine tool, sharpness of the cutting tool, and skill of the operator. Figure 6.3 indicates the range of tolerances to be expected for various machining operations. To use the table shown in the figure, first consider the size of the feature in the left column. Then go below the sizes in the left column to the type of machining operation used. The bar associated with that process indicates the range of tolerances in the row associated with the feature size. For instance, consider a feature that has a dimension of 2 inches. If broaching were used to create that feature, the chart indicates that the total tolerance would be .0004 to .0015, depending on the machining conditions. Thus, this dimension could be specified as 2.0000 ± .0002 up to

Size (in.)	Total Tolerance (in.)								
0.000-0.599	0.00015	0.0002	0.0003	0.0005	0.0008	0.0012	0.002	0.003	0.005
0.600-0.999	0.00015	0.00025	0.0004	0.0006	0.001	0.0015	0.0025	0.004	0.006
1.000-1.499	0.0002	0.0003	0.0005	0.0008	0.0012	0.002	0.003	0.005	0.008
1.500-2.799	0.00025	0.0004	0.0006	0.001	0.0015	0.0025	0.004	0.006	0.010
2.800-4.499	0.0003	0.0005	0.0008	0.0012	0.002	0.003	0.005	0.008	0.012
4.500-7.799	0.0004	0.0006	0.001	0.0015	0.0025	0.004	0.006	0.010	0.015
7.800-13.599	0.0005	0.0008	0.0012	0.002	0.003	0.005	0.008	0.012	0.025

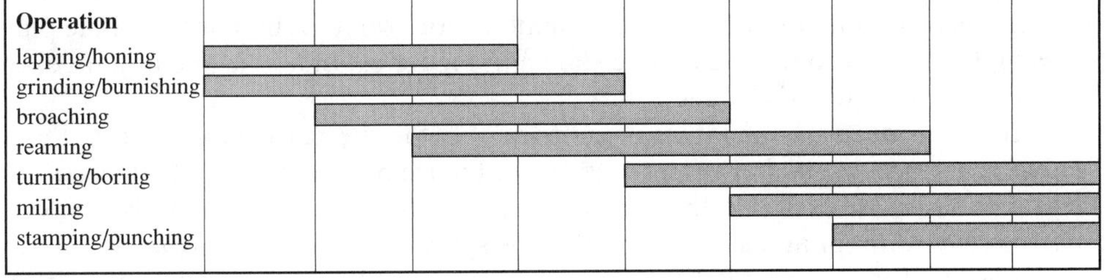

Operation

lapping/honing
grinding/burnishing
broaching
reaming
turning/boring
milling
stamping/punching

Figure 6.3
Range of tolerances for various machining operations.

2.0000 ± .0008 (rounding up). If the same piece were created on a milling machine, the tolerances would be .0025 to .010, indicating a dimension of 2.0000 ± .0013 up to 2.000 ± .005. If broaching were not available, we would have to be satisfied with the tolerances of a milling machine and adjust the design accordingly, if the milling tolerances are too large. If both broaching and milling were available, the criticality of the tolerance and the cost of manufacturing would drive the tolerance that would be specified on the drawing. (Broaching, a mass-production process, is usually more expensive than milling, so milling would be preferred if the milling tolerances are acceptable.) Tolerances for metric dimensioning can be determined by converting the values in Figure 6.3 to millimeters and rounding off the result to one less place to the right of the decimal point.

Typical tolerances on drills depend on the drill size. Standard drill sizes are fractional in increments of $\frac{1}{64}$ inch and range from $\frac{1}{16}$ inch to 4 inches. In addition, drills sizes are specified according to an alphanumeric code. The coded drill sizes range from 80 (.0135 inch) to 1 (.2280 inch) and from A (.234 inch) to Z (.413 inch). The dimensions for the coded drill sizes are widely available in engineering and machinist handbooks. In addition, the proper drill sizes for drilling holes that will be tapped are listed in these handbooks. The standard tolerances for drilled holes are given in Table 6.1.

Table 6.1 Standard Tolerances for Drilled Holes

Drill Size (In.)	Tolerance (In.)	
	Plus	Minus
0.0135 (80)–0.185 (13)	0.003	0.002
0.1875–0.246 (D)	0.004	0.002
0.250–0.750	0.005	0.002
0.7656–1.000	0.007	0.003
1.0156–2.000	0.010	0.004
2.0312–3.500	0.015	0.005

6.4 FITS

The degree of tightness or looseness between mating parts is known as the *fit*. This concept is most easily explained in terms of a shaft and a hole, although the concept can be applied to other mating parts in which an internal member is designed to fit within an external member. For example, a shaft that is .750 inch in diameter will fit into a hole that is .751 inch in diameter with .001 inch of clearance, but it will be too large for a hole that is .749 inch in diameter. But the situation is more complicated than this because the tolerances on the diameters of both the shaft and the hole play roles in the fit. Consider the example shown in Figure 6.4 of a hole and a shaft, each with a basic diameter of .750 inch.

In a *clearance fit*, the internal component fits in the mating part so that there is always a space or gap between the parts. In Figure 6.4, the largest shaft size for a clearance fit is .748 inch and the smallest hole size is .750 inch, so there is always a space or *clearance* of at least +.002 inch. This space is called the *allowance*. It is always positive for a clearance fit. The gap may be even larger. The smallest shaft in the largest hole results in an allowance of +.006 inch. A clearance fit is used when a shaft is meant to rotate or slide within the hole.

An *interference fit* occurs when the internal component is larger than the mating external member, so that the two parts will interfere with one another if they are assembled. For the interference fit in Figure 6.4, the smallest shaft, which is .753 inch, is too big to fit into the largest hole, which is only .752 inch. In this case, the allowance is −.001 inch, a negative number to indicate interference. This is known as the *least material condition*, or LMC, for which the least material for the shaft and the block with the hole are present. In other words, both the shaft and the portion of the block left over after the hole is cut are as small as possible. For the block, this corresponds to the largest hole. At the opposite extreme is the *maximum material condition*, or MMC, for which the maximum amount of material is present for the shaft and the block with the hole. For this condition, which corresponds to the largest shaft (.755 inch) and the smallest hole (.750 inch), the allowance is −.005 inch. To assemble these parts requires either using force to press the shaft into the hole, which is called a *press fit*, or using heating or cooling to stretch the hole or shrink the shaft. The latter are called *shrink fits*. They are often accomplished by heating the hole to expand it or cooling the shaft to shrink it, assembling the shaft in the hole, and then allowing the assembly to return to room temperature. Interference fits can be quite useful in design applications to mechanically fasten parts together without the use of fasteners or adhesive.

A *transition fit* results when the tolerances are such that the fit can be either a clearance fit or an interference fit when the parts are assembled. The transition fit in

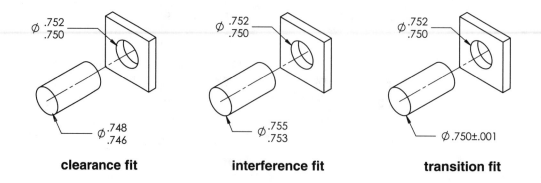

Figure 6.4
Clearance, interference, and transition fits.

clearance fit   **interference fit**   **transition fit**

Figure 6.4 is a clearance fit if the shaft has a dimension of .749 and the hole is .752 (the least material condition), but it is an interference fit if the shaft is .751 and the hole is .750 (the maximum material condition). Transition fits are sometimes used to position or locate one part with respect to another.

ANSI, ISO, and other organizations have issued engineering standards for a variety of types of shaft-in-hole fits to aid engineers in designing for particular applications. For instance, "running and sliding fits" prescribe the clearances for situations in which a shaft should rotate (running) or slide in a hole. There are a variety of running and sliding fits ranging from "close sliding fits" in which the clearance is quite small so that there is no perceptible play between the parts to "loose running fits" in which the clearance is quite large when accuracy is not essential. The engineering standard indicates the optimal clearance to be specified for the particular type of running or sliding condition that is required. There are also engineering standards for "locational fits," which are used to position one part with respect to another, and for "force and shrink fits" to fasten parts together.

6.5 SURFACE FINISH

All surfaces are rough and irregular on a microscopic scale. The roughness can be described in terms of asperities (peaks or ridges) and valleys. The irregularities of a surface are classified into **roughness** and **waviness**. Roughness describes the small-scale, somewhat random irregularity of a surface, while waviness describes a more regular variation in the surface that typically has a wavelength of 0.8 mm or more. The surface can be thought of as a roughness superimposed on waviness. The roughness and waviness can be measured in several ways, but the most common is with a profilometer, an instrument that drags a fine-pointed stylus over the surface and records the height of the stylus. The roughness is measured in terms of the roughness average (R_a). The roughness average is the average height of peaks above or valleys below the local surface height. More precisely, it is defined as the average of the absolute values of the deviation of the local surface height from the average height of the surface. This is equivalent to half the average of the peak-to-valley height. In addition, the **lay**, or predominant direction of the marks left by the machine tools, may be important in describing the surface.

The surface finish resulting from several machining and forming processes are shown in Figure 6.5. This figure shows the range of possible surface roughness averages (R_a) in both micrometers (1 μm $= 10^{-6}$ m) and microinches (1 μin $= 10^{-6}$ in). For instance, surfaces formed by drilling are likely to have a roughness from 12.5 μm down to 0.8 μm (500 μin down to 32 μin). Typically, the roughness is in the middle of the specified range, about 6.3 μm down to 1.6 μm for the case of drilling. In addition to the machining processes described in Section 6.3, the following processes are also included in Figure 6.5:

> **Sawing:** Cutting material by moving a toothed blade through the material.
> **Polishing:** Removal of scratches and tool marks on a surface using a belt or rotating wheel of soft material such as cloth or leather, often with a fine abrasive.
> **Sand Casting:** Forming a part by pouring molten metal into a mold made of sand.
> **Forging:** Shaping of metal to a desired form by pressing or hammering, usually with the metal hot.
> **Permanent Mold Casting:** Forming a part by pouring molten metal into a permanent mold.

	Roughness Average, R_a												
Micrometers (µm)	50	25	12.5	6.3	3.2	1.6	0.80	0.40	0.20	0.10	0.05	0.025	0.012
Microinches (µin.)	2000	1000	500	250	125	63	32	16	8	4	2	1	0.5

Sawing
Drilling
Milling
Broaching
Reaming
Turning/Boring
Grinding
Honing
Lapping
Polishing
Sand casting
Forging
Perm. mold casting

Figure 6.5
Surface roughness for various machining operations.

To put the roughness averages in perspective, consider that a 0.10-µm roughness is a mirrorlike surface, free from visible marks of any kind. A 1.6-µm roughness is a high-quality, smooth machined finish. A 6.3-µm roughness is the ordinary finish from typical machining operations.

The surface finish may be specified on a drawing using the special symbols touching the surface or with a leader line to the surface as shown in Figure 6.6. For the top surface, the roughness is specified as 1.2 µm, corresponding to a high-quality, smooth machine finish. The surface finish symbol on the right side of the object includes a horizontal bar that indicates that material removal by machining is required for this surface. The surface finish symbol on the left side of the object indicates that material removal from this side is prohibited. This surface must be the one resulting from the original process used to produce the surface, such as casting, forging, or injection molding.

Other notations can be added to the surface roughness symbol. A number to the left of the surface finish mark describes the material removal allowance indicating the amount of stock material to be removed by machining. A symbol to the right of the surface roughness mark indicates the lay, or predominant direction of machining marks: perpendicular, parallel, circular, or radial. Other notations can be used to specify the waviness. Details of surface finish notation are available in engineering and machinist handbooks.

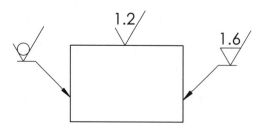

Figure 6.6
Surface roughness symbols.

6.6 GEOMETRIC DIMENSIONING AND TOLERANCING

Ideally, engineering drawings should be unambiguous in their interpretation. In many cases, stating dimensions and tolerances provides adequate information so that the part can be manufactured to ensure interchangeability of parts and optimal performance. But sometimes the traditional dimensioning using the plus and minus scheme does not adequately describe the geometry of the part. For instance, consider the part shown in Figure 6.7. The dimension shown in the drawing could have several possible interpretations. For instance, the dimension at the top edge could be 14.9 mm while the dimension at the bottom edge could be 15.1 mm, resulting in a trapezoidal part instead of a rectangular part. Or the right edge of the part could be bowed so that the part is 15.1 mm wide at the top and bottom, but 14.9 mm wide at the middle. As a result, the part would not fit flush against another flat surface even though the part is 15 ± .1 mm wide at any particular location. In both of these cases, the geometry of the part is not described fully by the plus and minus tolerances on the dimension.

A system known as *geometric dimensioning and tolerancing* is used to prevent such ambiguities in the design by presenting the design intent more clearly. Geometric dimensioning and tolerancing supplements the traditional dimensioning system with specifications that describe the geometry of the part to enhance the interpretation of the drawing. This system is used to indicate dimensions critical to a part's function and ensure part interchangeability. Items related to geometric dimensioning and tolerancing are indicated on a drawing by a feature symbol consisting of a frame or box around the information describing the geometry. A complete discussion of geometric dimensioning and tolerancing is beyond the scope of this book—there are entire books on the subject. Nevertheless, several of the key aspects and applications of geometric dimensioning and tolerancing are presented here to familiarize the reader with the basic terminology and symbols that are used.

The various types of tolerances and the characteristics that they describe are indicated in Figure 6.8. Each has its own symbol that is used on a drawing. Perhaps the easiest type of geometric tolerances to understand are the *form tolerances*, which describe the shape of a single feature. For instance, straightness indicates the limits on how much a surface or axis can bow with respect to a straight line. Figure 6.9 shows the *straightness* specification for a surface. A feature control box with the straightness symbol (a horizontal bar) and a numerical dimension are connected by a leader line to the surface. The interpretation is that the upper surface must be straight enough so that all points on the surface are within the tolerance zone of

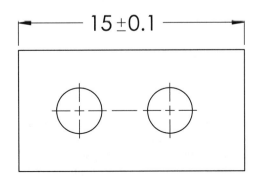

Figure 6.7
Ambiguity can result from dimensioning as shown.

	TYPE OF TOLERANCE	CHARACTERISTIC	SYMBOL
FOR INDIVIDUAL FEATURES	FORM	STRAIGHTNESS	—
		FLATNESS	▱
		CIRCULARITY (ROUNDNESS)	○
		CYLINDRICITY	⌭
FOR INDIVIDUAL OR RELATED FEATURES	PROFILE	PROFILE OF A LINE	⌒
		PROFILE OF A SURFACE	⌓
FOR RELATED FEATURES	ORIENTATION	ANGULARITY	∠
		PERPENDICULARITY	⊥
		PARALLELISM	//
	LOCATION	POSITION	⌖
		CONCENTRICITY	◎
		SYMMETRY	⌯
	RUNOUT	CIRCULAR RUNOUT	↗
		TOTAL RUNOUT	↗↗

Figure 6.8
Types of tolerances and their symbols.

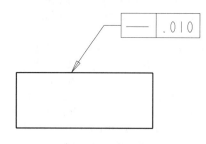

Drawing Notation

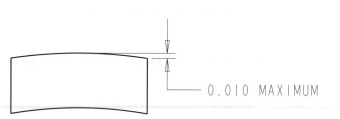

0.010 MAXIMUM

Interpretation

Figure 6.9
Straightness specification.

0.010 mm. An example of a *flatness* specification is shown in Figure 6.10. The parallelogram symbol with a numerical dimension in a feature control box indicates that the planar surface must lie between two parallel planes 0.20 mm apart. Other single feature specifications include *circularity* or *roundness* (for circular features to be within a tolerance zone defined by two concentric circles), and *cylindricity* (for

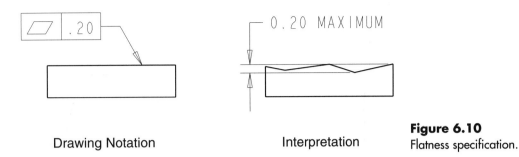

Drawing Notation   Interpretation

Figure 6.10
Flatness specification.

cylindrical features to be within a tolerance zone defined by two concentric cylinders). Closely related to form tolerances are ***profile tolerances***, which define the acceptable deviation of the outline of an object (profile) from that specified in the drawing. These tolerances define a zone on either side of the true profile shown on the drawing within which the line or surface should remain. Profile tolerances can be applied to either a line or a surface.

    Orientation tolerances prescribe the relation between features. ***Parallelism*** controls the degree to which a surface is parallel to a reference plane, or datum plane. In Figure 6.11, the horizontal datum plane that coincides with the bottom edge of the part is identified with a box around B attached to the bottom edge. The parallelism feature symbol (parallel lines), the numerical tolerance, and the reference datum plane are included in a feature control box with a leader line to the surface to which the tolerance applies. In this case, the upper surface must be within 0.10 mm of parallel to datum plane B. ***Perpendicularity*** with respect to a datum plane is indicated in a similar way, as shown in Figure 6.12. Here the vertical plane must be perpendicular to datum plane A to within 0.20 mm. In this example, an alternative notation for specifying datum plane A is used. The datum plane symbol used in Figure 6.12 is common, but the datum plane symbol used in Figure 6.11 and Figure 6.13 is preferred. The datum plane symbol can be applied in several different ways as shown in Figure 6.11 and Figure 6.13. Several other relations between features can be specified, including the tolerance zone for ***angularity*** from a datum plane or axis, the tolerance zone for ***concentricity*** of a surface of revolution with respect to an axis, the tolerance zone for ***symmetry*** with respect to a datum plane, and the tolerance zone for ***runout***, which describes the circularity with respect to an axis of revolution.

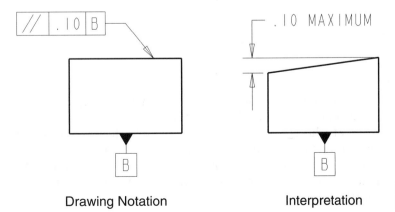

Drawing Notation   Interpretation

Figure 6.11
Parallelism specification.

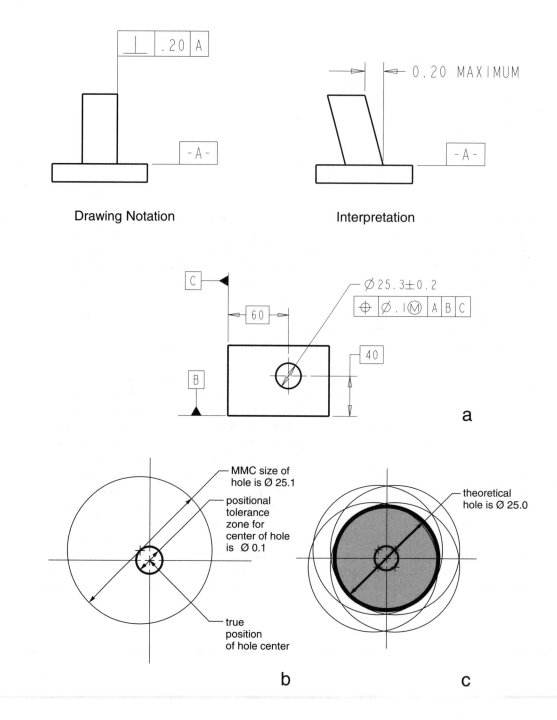

Figure 6.12
Perpendicularity specification.

Drawing Notation

Interpretation

Figure 6.13
Positional tolerances.

The most difficult concept in geometric dimensioning and tolerancing is the concept of *positional tolerances*. It is demonstrated most easily in indicating the position of a hole, as shown in Figure 6.13a. In this case, the ultimate goal is to have a circular open area (hole) that is at least 25.0 mm in diameter with its center exactly at the position indicated in the drawing. Note that even though we want a 25.0-mm hole, the hole is dimensioned as 25.3 mm in the drawing. The reason for this will shortly become evident.

Rather than describing the position of the hole with a plus-or-minus tolerance, the ideal position of the hole is prescribed. The boxes around the 40 mm and 60 mm dimensions indicate that they are basic ***true-position dimensions***, which describe the perfect position of the center of the hole. Then the feature control box below the dimension of the hole shows how close the center of the hole should be to the true position. In this case, the hole should be within a circular tolerance zone with a diameter of 0.1 mm of the true position (indicated by the plus in the circle within the feature control box followed by Ø.1). The reference datum planes are also included in the feature control box. Datum plane A is the surface of the part in the plane of the page. Datum planes B and C are references for the true-position dimensions of 40 mm and 60 mm. These three mutually perpendicular datum planes provide a reference point for the positional tolerance of the hole.

The positional tolerance zone for the center of the hole is shown in Figure 6.13b. The "true position of the hole center" is based on the 40 and 60 mm dimensions. Around this center is a circle with a diameter of 0.1 mm (not drawn to scale in Figure 6.13b) that defines the "positional tolerance zone." The center of the actual hole must be within this circle. For instance, an acceptable hole would be a 25.1-mm-diameter hole with its center on the edge of this circular tolerance zone, as shown in Figure 6.13b.

The circled M in the feature control box in Figure 6.13a indicates that the 0.1-mm circular positional tolerance zone is applied at the ***maximum material condition*** (MMC). For a hole, the maximum material condition is the smallest acceptable dimension of the hole, because this is the situation in which the most material would be present. For the part in Figure 6.13a, the diameter of the hole for the maximum material condition is 25.1 mm, given a dimension of 25.3 ± 0.2 for the diameter of the hole. Thus, the circle representing a hole with its center on the edge of the positional tolerance zone has a diameter of 25.1 mm, as shown in Figure 6.13b. Of course, the 25.1-mm-diameter hole could be anywhere within the positional tolerance zone or on its edge. Three more 25.1-mm-diameter circles are drawn in Figure 6.13c in addition to the original 25.1-mm circle. The centers of all four circles are on the edge of the positional tolerance zone. Note that there is a circle that lies inside all of the 25.1-mm-diameter circles, which is called the ***theoretical hole***. It is relatively straightforward to find the diameter of the theoretical hole, based on the positional tolerance zone for the center of the hole and the MMC size of the hole. The radius of the theoretical hole is the distance from the true position of the hole center to the nearest portion of any one of the MMC circles. Here the theoretical hole has a diameter of 25.0 mm. In fact, the theoretical hole always has a diameter equal to the diameter for the maximum material condition minus the diameter of the positional tolerance (in this case, 25.1 mm − 0.1 mm = 25.0 mm).

The key result is that if the hole diameter is within the specified tolerance (25.3 ± .2 mm) and the center of the hole is within the positional tolerance zone (.1 mm), there will always be a circular opening in the part with a diameter of at least 25.0 mm. Now assume that the hole must mate with a circular pin that is positioned at the true center of the hole and is exactly 25.0 mm in diameter. Given the dimensioning scheme in Figure 6.13a, the pin will always align with the theoretical hole and fit through the theoretical hole, even if the actual hole is not positioned so that its center is exactly at the true position of the hole center. Of course, the theoretical hole is based on the maximum material condition (smallest hole allowed). If the hole is at the large end of the acceptable tolerance, 25.5 mm in diameter, circles drawn in Figure 6.13c will be larger. But the theoretical hole will still be open for the pin. Likewise, if the circles drawn in Figure 6.13c are not on the edge of the positional tolerance zone, but inside of the zone, the entire theoretical hole will still be open for the pin. Thus, defining the position and diameter of the hole as in Figure 6.13a forces the existence of an open area (theoretical hole) that is at least 25.0 mm in diameter and centered at the true position of the hole center.

The maximum material condition reflects the practical aspect of assembly. Consider two parts that are bolted together with several bolts. If the bolt holes are not accurately positioned, not all of the bolts can be inserted. Either drilling out the holes to make them larger or using smaller diameter bolts fixes the problem. The idea of the maximum material condition is to capture these trade-offs. The maximum material condition indicates the inner boundary (the theoretical hole) for the actual hole. The boundary of the actual hole must always be outside of this inner boundary. In this way, a bolt or pin that is positioned at the true position of the hole will always fit through the actual hole. Likewise, the least material condition, or largest hole size, can be used to define a theoretical circle within which the actual hole will be. The boundary for the actual hole must lie inside of the theoretical circle as defined by the LMC. Further information regarding geometric dimensioning and tolerancing is provided in engineering handbooks and graphics textbooks.

KEY TERMS

Actual size	Geometric dimensioning	Profile tolerance
Allowance	and tolerancing	Roughness
Angularity	Interchangeable parts	Roundness
Basic size	Interference fit	Runout
Bilateral tolerance	Jig	Shrink fit
Chain dimensioning	Least material condition	Single limit dimension
Circularity	Limit dimensions	Straightness
Clearance fit	Maximum material condi-	Target size
Concentricity	tion	Theoretical hole
Cylindricity	Nominal size	Tolerance
Datum dimensioning	Orientation tolerances	Tolerance accumulation
Fit	Parellelism	Tolerance stackup
Flatness	Perpendicularity	Transition fit
Form tolerances	Plus and minus dimensions	True-position dimension
Gauge	Positional tolerances	Unilateral tolerance
General tolerances	Press fit	

PROBLEMS

6.1 The part shown in Figure 6.14 is made by using a very accurate milling machine by a skilled machinist. The hole is reamed. Specify plus and minus tolerances for each dimension, assuming that it is critical to hold all dimensions as close as possible to those specified. Use four digits past the decimal point to specify the tolerances, even though typical practice would be to specify only three digits past the decimal point. Dimensions are in inches.

6.2 The part shown in Figure 6.14 is made by an unskilled student using an old milling machine in a university student shop. The hole is drilled. Specify plus and minus tolerances for each dimension that are reasonable for these conditions. Use four digits past the decimal point to specify the tolerances, even though typical practice would be to specify only three digits past the decimal point. Dimensions are in inches.

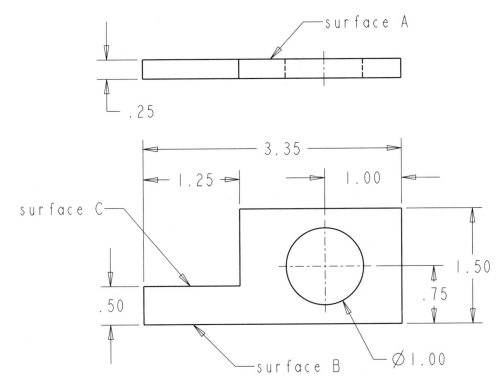

Figure 6.14

6.3 Sketch or draw using CAD a view of the object shown in Figure 6.15. Specify the horizontal dimension of the steps, using chain dimensioning from the left end. The length of each horizontal section from left to right is .50, .75, 1.25, and .25 inches. The object is .50 inches thick, .25 inches high at the left end, and 1.00 inch high at the right end. Base the plus and minus dimensions on the worst expected tolerances for milling. What are the maximum and minimum dimensions for the overall horizontal length of the object? Use four digits past the decimal point to specify the tolerances, even though typical practice would be to specify only three digits past the decimal point.

6.4 Sketch or draw using CAD a view of the object shown in Figure 6.15. Specify the horizontal dimension of the steps using datum dimensioning from the left end. The length of each horizontal section from left to right is .50, .75, 1.25,

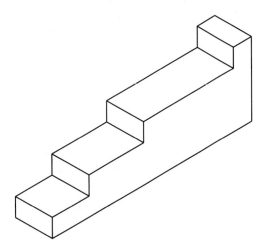

Figure 6.15

and .25 inches. The object is .50 inches thick, .25 inches high at the left end, and 1.00 inch high at the right end. Base the plus and minus dimensions on the best expected tolerances for milling. What are the maximum and minimum dimensions for the overall horizontal length of the object? Use four digits past the decimal point to specify the tolerances, even though typical practice would be to specify only three digits past the decimal point.

6.5 Sketch or draw using CAD a side view of the shaft shown in Figure 6.16. Specify the horizontal dimension of each section of the shaft using chain dimensioning from the left end. The length of each horizontal section from left to right is .75, 2.00, .50, 1.25, and 3.00 inches. The small diameter is .50 inches; the large diameter is 1.00 inch. Base the plus and minus dimensions on the best expected tolerances for turning. What are the maximum and minimum dimensions for the overall horizontal length of the object? Use four digits past the decimal point to specify the tolerances, even though typical practice would be to specify only three digits past the decimal point.

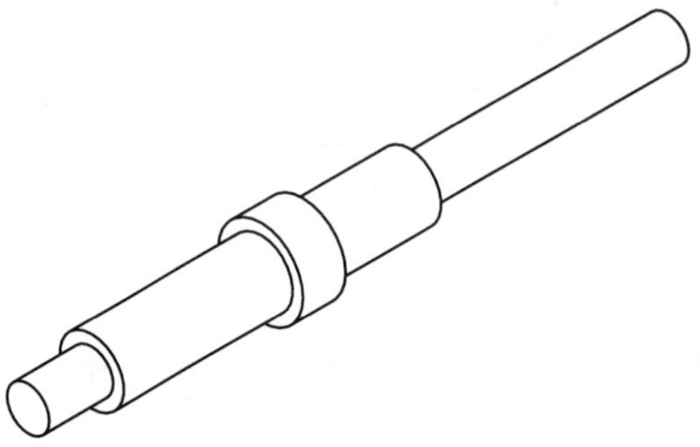

Figure 6.16

6.6 Sketch or draw using CAD a side view of the shaft shown in Figure 6.16. Specify the horizontal dimension of each section of the shaft using datum dimensioning from the left end. The length of each horizontal section from left to right is .75, 2.00, .50, 1.25, and 3.00 inches. The small diameter is .50 inches; the large diameter is 1.00 inch. Base the plus and minus dimensions on the worst expected tolerances for turning. What are the maximum and minimum dimensions for the length from the left end to the left edge of the largest diameter section? Use four digits past the decimal point to specify the tolerances, even though typical practice would be to specify only three digits past the decimal point.

6.7 Determine whether the following are a clearance fit, interference fit, or transition fit. For clearance and interference fits, determine the allowance.

(a) a hole is 1.500 + .002/−.000, and the mating shaft is 1.498 ± .001.

(b) a hole is 1.250 + .000/−.002, and the mating shaft is 1.250 ± .001.

(c) a slot is .625 ± .001 wide and the mating tab to fit in the slot is .628 ± .001.

6.8 A tube with an inner diameter of 3.500 ± .002 and a wall thickness of 0.188 +.001/−.002 fits into a circular slot. The tolerance on the inner diameter and outer diameter of the slot is ±.002.

(a) What should the basic size be for the inner diameter of the slot if there is to be a clearance fit with an allowance of .002?

(b) What should the basic size be for the outer diameter of the slot if there is to be an interference fit with an allowance of −.001?

6.9 Draw the appropriate surface finish symbol for

(a) a surface roughness typical for drilling.

(b) a surface roughness typical for grinding.

(c) the best possible surface roughness for milling with material removal required.

(d) a surface finish of 12.5 microns with material removal prohibited.

6.10 Sketch the appropriate geometric dimensioning and tolerancing form for

(a) a straight edge so that all points on the surface are within a tolerance zone of 0.020 mm.

(b) a surface that is flat to within 0.015 mm.

(c) a surface that is parallel to datum plane C to within 0.20 mm.

(d) a surface that is perpendicular to datum plane B to within 0.10 mm.

(e) a hole that is perpendicular to datum plane B to within 0.12 mm.

6.11 The part shown in Figure 6.17 is dimensioned in millimeters using the traditional coordinate method. Sketch or use CAD to draw the same views of the part and dimension. Use geometric dimensioning and tolerancing procedures so that the following functional requirements are met:

• Set surfaces A and B as datum planes.

• Surface A is flat to within 0.15 mm.

• The upper edge in the front view from which the holes are located vertically is perpendicular to surface B to within 0.20 mm. Set this edge as datum plane C.

• The edge-forming surface A in the top view is straight to within 0.05 mm.

• The 10-, 15-, and 40-mm dimensions are true-position dimensions.

• The 5-, 30-, and 50-mm dimensions must be held to the tightest possible tolerance that can be achieved using milling. Convert the dimensions to inches to determine the tolerances to two places after the decimal point

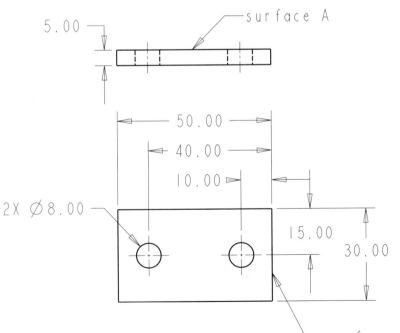

Figure 6.17

(round as necessary). Specify the tolerances as plus and minus dimensions in millimeters.

- The holes have a tolerance of ±0.05 mm. The theoretical hole size is 8.00 mm.
- The holes are located within 0.15 mm of the true position at the maximum material condition.

6.12 The part shown in Figure 6.14 is dimensioned in inches using the traditional coordinate method. Sketch or use CAD to draw the same views of the part and dimension. Use geometric dimensioning and tolerancing procedures so that the following functional requirements are met:

- Set surfaces A and B as datum planes. Set the right edge as datum plane D.
- Surface A is flat to within .005 inch.
- The hole is perpendicular to surface A to within .010 inch. (Place this tolerance just below the dimension.)
- Surface C is parallel to surface B to within .012 inch.
- The .75-inch and 1.00-inch dimensions for the location of the hole are true-position dimensions.
- The 1.50-inch and 3.35-inch dimensions must be held to the tightest possible tolerance that can be achieved using milling. (Use three digits past the decimal point for the tolerances.)
- The hole has a tolerance of ±.002 inch. The theoretical hole size is 1.000 inch.
- The hole is located within .004 inch of the true position at the maximum material condition.

6.13 The part shown in Figure 6.18 is dimensioned in millimeters using the traditional coordinate method. Sketch or use CAD to draw the same views of the

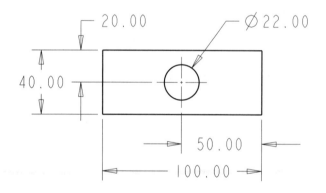

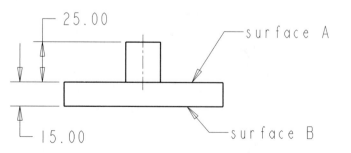

Figure 6.18

part and dimension. Use geometric dimensioning and tolerancing procedures so that the following functional requirements are met:

- Set surface A as a datum plane.
- Surface B is flat to within 0.10 mm.
- Surface B is parallel to surface A to within 0.05 mm.
- The 40-mm and 100-mm dimensions need only be held to the loosest possible tolerance that can be achieved using milling. (Convert the dimensions to inches to determine the tolerances. Specify the tolerances as plus and minus dimensions in millimeters.)

REFERENCES

ASME Y14.5M-1994, Dimensioning and Tolerancing. New York, NY: American Society of Mechanical Engineers, 1995.

G. R. Bertoline, *Introduction to Graphics Communications for Engineers.* New York, NY: Mc-Graw- Hill, 1999.

P. J. Booker, *A History of Engineering Drawing.* London, England: Northgate Publishing Co. Ltd., 1979.

S. H. Chasen, Historical Highlights of Interactive Computer Graphics. *Mechanical Engineering,* November 1981, 32–41.

G. E. Dieter, *Engineering Design: A Materials and Processing Approach.* New York, NY: Mc-Graw-Hill, 1991.

A. R. Eide, R. D. Jenison, L. H. Mashaw, L. L. Northup, and C. G. Sanders, *Engineering Graphics Fundamentals.* New York, NY: McGraw-Hill, 1985.

J. Encarnacao and E. G. Schlechtendahl, *Computer Aided Design.* Berlin, Germany: Springer-Verlag, 1983.

E. S. Ferguson, *Engineering and the Mind's Eye.* Cambridge MA: The MIT Press, 1992.

E. S. Ferguson, The Mind's Eye: Nonverbal Thought in Technology. *Science* 197:827–836, 1977.

F. E. Giesecke, A. Mitchell, H. C. Spencer, I. L. Hill, R. O. Loving, J. T. Dygdon, J. E. Novak, and S. Lockhart, *Engineering Graphics.* Upper Saddle River, NJ: Prentice Hall, 1998.

K. Hanks, *Rapid Viz: A New Method for the Rapid Visualization of Ideas.* Menlo Park, CA: Crisp Publications, 1990.

C. M. Hoffman, *Geometric and Solid Modeling.* San Mateo, CA: Morgan Kaufmann Publishers, Inc., 1989.

S. Pugh, *Total Design.* Reading, MA: Addison Wesley, 1990.

D. G. Ullman, *The Mechanical Design Process,* 2nd Edition. New York, NY: McGraw-Hill, 1997.

D. G. Ullman, S. Wood, and D. Craig, The Importance of Drawing in the Mechanical Design Process. *Computers and graphics,* 14:263–274, 1990.

W. R. D. Wilson, Course Notes for ME B40: Introduction to Mechanical Design and Manufacturing. Northwestern University, March 1998.

Index